THE ULTIMATE LIFE SKILL

Happiness is the meaning and purpose of life, the whole aim and end of human existence
Aristotle

By Dr Barrie Hopson and Mike Scally

Live Happier Limited
17 Hunslet Road, Leeds, LS10 1QN

First Edition Copyright
© Barrie Hopson and Mike Scally

First Published 2012
Printed by Lulu.com

ISBN: 978-1-3000674-3-6

Published by Livehappier Limited
Typeset by First 10 Digital Limited

Dr Barrie Hopson

Current portfolio career includes:

- Director of Live Happier Ltd.
- Chairman of Axia Interactive Media.
- Writer and presenter. Written 39 books including the bestselling 12 Steps to Success through Service, The Lifeskills Teaching Programmes, Build Your Own Rainbow, The Rainbow Years: the Pluses of Being 50+ and an accompanying website. The latter were all co-authored with Mike Scally. Most recent book (2009) was And What Do You Do? 10 Steps to Creating a Portfolio Career, with Katie Ledger www.portfoliocareers.net.
- He set up the Counselling and Career Development Unit (CCDU) at Leeds University in 1976.
- Founded Lifeskills International with Mike Scally and was joint CEO and Chairman until 1999.
- Fellow of the British Psychological Society.

Barrie has devoted his professional life *to helping people become architects of their own future.* **As such it has been a natural development to begin to define and develop the life skills required to be able to live happier.**

livehappier.com

authors

Mike is enjoying a creative retirement with great enthusiasm for learning about happiness and working with others who are passionate to build happier communities and happier lives.

Mike Scally

- After years in teaching Mike joined Barrie and became deputy Director of the CCDU at Leeds University.
- Mike and Barrie went on to found and grow Lifeskills International Ltd and Citizen Connect, people development organisations.
- Mike consulted with and trained for organisations internationally, in Europe, Australia, Canada, Hong Kong, Scandinavia, Uganda and Brazil, and has a particular interest in making his experience available to agencies working for development in the poorest areas of the world.
- Mike has written over 30 books and has led workshops at many international conferences on the themes of Life Skills Teaching, Culture Change, Building Customer-driven Organisations, Service Excellence, Career Development and Self-managed Learning.
- He has a grown up family of six children and seven grandchildren to whom he would like to gift the insights of happier living.

Please Note

All the material in this book is offered in good faith and is intended to raise awareness and inform life choices that lead to happier lives. It has been conscientiously researched and assembled, but is offered very much as an inspiration to everyday living and individual decision-making and NOT as a programme approved by medical, mental health or any professional therapeutic bodies. Users will make their own, informed decisions about the application to their unique lives and the authors cannot be held responsible for any outcomes that result from thoughts arising nor action taken on the basis of the content of this book.

 livehappier.com

contents

Introduction	2
Relationships and happiness	44
Work and happiness	90
Money and happiness	144
Health and happiness	170
Leisure and happiness	208
Learning and happiness	234
Home and happiness	262
Spirituality and happiness	284
What next?	312
Acknowledgements	334

live happier: the ultimate life skill

introduction

don't just read it! use it!

This is a book to be 'used' and not just read. Capture your realisations! Act on them!

An Introduction To Living Happier

1.1 What We Believe

We believe that the 'science of happiness' can make a significant contribution to enhancing human happiness. Our role is to play a part in that movement.

In committing to that mission, we are driven by the following values and beliefs:

- all individuals have vast, and largely untapped, potential;
- 2+2=5 (when we are connected with others we can achieve even more than we can separately);
- love, care, creativity, integrity, respect and mutuality are conducive to human development and happier lives, and should be demonstrated in our lives and in our work;
- communities which combine their skills, talents, experience and wisdom have a vast capacity to exponentially enhance happiness in many lives;
- 'the good life', a key component of 'living happier', is one which contributes to 'the common good', in which each of us uses our uniqueness and our talents to enhance the happiness not just of ourselves, but also that of our families and friends, our communities, our country and our world;
- we can all make significant contributions to building happier relationships, happier communities, happier nations by seeking always to being part of the solution rather than being part of the problem.

1.2 What are Life Skills?

In the 1970s we introduced 'life skills'[1] to the world of UK education.[1] Our proposal was that, alongside the academic curriculum, we ought to be teaching young people the skills that would enable them to live effectively in whatever future faced them. We were saying that while exams and qualifications opened career doors, they did not and do not fully equip us for the essential tasks and challenges of our lives ahead. Whether those lives are to be happy and successful will depend more on how skilled and effective we are in a range of life roles as learners, workers, partners, friends, parents and citizens, rather than on a sheaf of exam certificates.

In the 15,000 hours that young people spent in schooling we claimed there was a place to teach:

- a recognition that we are each unique and have the capacity to shape our lives for the better and help others to do the same;
- that a belief in ourselves and a respect for others is a great basis for building the future; and
- that skills such as relationship-building, decision-making, problem-solving, managing change, job-seeking, team-working, time-management, effective communication, health maintenance, managing negative feelings, being assertive not aggressive, and many others we identified, should be learnt alongside literacy and numeracy.

---

1 B. Hopson and M. Scally, Lifeskills Teaching (McGraw-Hill, London, 1981).

introduction

Education, we said, should be about more than just information giving, storing and regurgitating if it is to prepare us for a fast-moving, ever-changing world and lives that will see futures we can currently hardly predict. Our Lifeskills Teaching Programmes[2] were published and used widely in schools, colleges, youth work, community groups and adult education.

Eventually, many major companies and organisations became interested in the idea of developing self-management skills in adults, to increase their autonomy and flexibility. Our company Lifeskills International Ltd pioneered career and life-planning workshops to give people the 'tools' to make their lives 'more like they wanted them to be'. These workshops became prominent parts of Human Resources (HR) provision over many years.

It is probably fair to say that there are few challenges and crises in the human situation that are to do with a lack of information. We are creating data at an incredible, exponential rate. Human happiness, however, is much more to do with our ability to do the following:

- build relationships;
- cooperate with others;
- work effectively;
- solve problems;
- think and act independently and responsibly;
- predict and plan;
- take decisions and manage consequences;
- continue learning, especially from experience;
- accept diversity;
- manage change;
- mature through life stages; and
- maintain our health and well-being, and support others to do the same.

2 Lifeskills Teaching Programmes Nos. 1, 2, 3 and 4 (Lifeskills International, 1980–88).

In short our ability to 'live happier' and support others in doing the same will very much depend on our 'life skills'.

So now it seems we have come full circle. Now we have the opportunity to spread the word and provide the 'tools' to enable more of us to 'live happier' lives. Enhancing happiness in our own life and helping others do the same is surely the 'ultimate life skill'.

1.3 Helping You and the World to Live Happier

Would you like to be happier in your work, in your relationships, in any or indeed in all aspects of life? Hardly anybody would say 'no' to that would they?

Happiness is surely the most universal pursuit. Some pursue greater wealth, believing it will make them 'happy', some seek promotion, some want new relationships, new jobs, a bigger house, children, adventure, travel, etc., but essentially they believe such a 'change' would make them 'happier'. The ultimate quest, via various goals, is for happiness.

'You can't be happy alone. You can't be happy all the time. You can be happier than you are.'
Dan Gilbert, - Psychologist[3]

introduction

In this book you can:

- review your own level of 'happiness';
- learn what scientific research from the world of 'Positive Psychology' can teach us all about 'happiness';
- explore eight key arenas of your life – relationships, work, health, money, leisure, learning, home, spirituality;
- discover how the eight arenas contribute (or don't at the moment) to your 'happiness' level;
- find a treasure trove of resources that can provide you with signposts in the 'pursuit of happiness'.

This is a Work Book

This book is meant to be more than a compilation of the best research from the world of Positive Psychology. It will give you a great deal of information on 'the science of happiness' but it will also ask you to reflect and to act on what you make of what you read.

No learning programme can dictate what is best for someone as unique as you. There has never been anyone with your combination of genes, upbringing, education, experiences, thoughts, values, contacts and relationships. So what you will find in the book are clues and options for you to consider, not prescriptions.

Where you will find 'answers' will be in the thoughts that the material stimulates in you. At intervals you may experience a real insight or, if you like, an 'Aha! moment'. Be alert to things about yourself and your life that occur to you as you work and use them to help you live happier.

You will regularly be asked to write in your thoughts and record your insights in response to what you have been reading. Print off the 'write-in' pages or use a notebook. These jottings will be important clues to things you want to work on, change or achieve, to help you and possibly others you are close to, to live happier.

3   D Gilbert, Stumbling on Happiness (Vintage, London, 2006)

Be alert to the things you become aware of about yourself, about your preferences, your aspirations and ambitions as you work through the activities or reflect on them later.

When it comes to the final stage, 'Where do you go from here?', we will ask you to re-visit what you have noted and use this data as an aid to set yourself objectives. If the write-in spaces are not sufficient use a digital or paper alternative.

Working with Someone Else:

We strongly hope that many of you will use this opportunity to connect with others working their way through the book. Sharing your thinking with others can help you refine and clarify your ideas. Also, their reactions, responses, and challenges are likely to be valuable and stimulating – and provide you with even more food for thought.

It can sometimes be enlightening to involve family, friends and colleagues in contributing their perspectives as you work on some of the activities. It could also be scary!

act on your realisations

This is a book to be 'used' and not just read. Capture your realisations! Act on them!

1.4 Living Happier in Life's Arenas

The aim is not to strive for 'happiness' full stop. Full-time, unchanging happiness is not achievable in life. Expecting it can lead to frustration and disappointment when we experience the 'low points' that every life will bring. The key is to develop the awareness and the 'life skills' that will enable us to 'live happier' more of the time and help those around us to do the same.

We invite you to examine the eight key arenas of life. For each one, we ask what could help you to live happier in that arena?

Each arena begins with an introduction to the topic and what the science can tell us about this. This is followed by activities, each of which will suggest some life skills that you might choose to develop to help you live happier in that particular arena of your life.

So, welcome to the adventure, join the quest, get involved, boost your happiness levels and help others to do the same!

'The Constitution only gives people the right to "pursue happiness". You have to catch it for yourself!' Benjamin Franklin

1.5 How Happy are You Now?

If someone asks you how happy you are, how would you answer? Would it be just a gut reaction or would you be more analytical of how you are feeling right now in the different areas of your life, your 'life arenas'?

It is good to review periodically just how we are doing. For example, we might be feeling overall not too happy with our life this morning. However, by reviewing each part of it we may realise that there is one area that is making us miserable, whereas, most or even all of the other arenas are fine. This is a reality check on our overall level of happiness.

introduction

How would you rate your happiness in each of the life arenas right now? Rate from 1-10 with 10 being happiest. For example, someone might score like this:

Relationships	5
Work	8
Money	8
Health	8
Leisure	7
Learning	3
Home	8
Spirituality	7
Average	6.75

Through this analysis this person would realise they are very happy with work, money, home and health. They are relatively OK with leisure and spirituality. But, clearly, they do have problems with some aspects of their relationships and really feel that they are not learning anything new. So although the average is 6.75 we can still feel unhappy because one or two arenas are problematic for us. Analysing our life arenas in this way can help put things into perspective.

live happier: the ultimate life skill

Do this for yourself.

Rate your happiness in each of these arenas right now from 1-10 with 10 being highest.

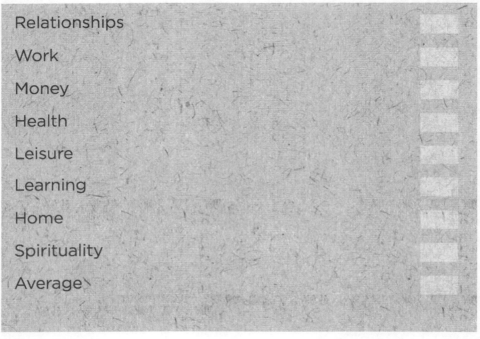

Relationships
Work
Money
Health
Leisure
Learning
Home
Spirituality
Average

rate your happiness here

introduction

What do you think this is telling you about how you are living your life right now and your levels of happiness in each arena?

Which would you say were the two happiest periods in your life so far? (Highlight)

	21–25,	46–50,
Childhood	26–30,	51–60,
10–13,	31–35,	61–70,
14–17,	36–40,	71–80,
18–20,	41–45,	over–80

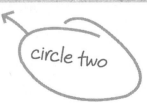

What made those periods the happiest?

Each chapter will offer you data and activities to help you consider how happy you are in each arena, and will invite you to explore what you might do to live happier.

introduction

Before going further let's examine just what we mean by 'happiness'.

We will begin by asking you what you think.

1.6 What is 'Happiness'?

What do *you* think? (Highlight the box that applies to you)

	Yes	No
1. Is 'happiness' achievable?		
2. Does 'happiness' mean the same thing to everybody?		
3. Is 'happiness' the purpose of life?		
4. Is 'happiness' related to wealth?		
5. Is 'happiness' just a modern fad?		
6. Is 'happiness' genetic?		
7. Is 'happiness' all in the mind?		
8. Is 'happiness' a political issue?		
9. Is 'happiness' just a myth or a mystery?		
10. Is 'happiness' contagious or infectious?		
11. Is 'happiness' just lots of pleasure?		
12. Can we learn to 'live happier'?		

livehappier.com

introduction

1. Is 'happiness' achievable?

Nobody is 'happy' all of the time. We are 'happier' sometimes, less happy other times. Living 'happier' is probably a more useful goal than seeking once and for all 'happiness'. At any one time we will feel to be somewhere between:

This will also vary for different periods in our life.

In other words, our level of 'happiness' rises and falls over time as a result of many factors internal and external to us. Our aim should be to raise the level, to live 'happier' by developing the awareness and skills to enable us to do just that. And ideally be able to help others do the same.

Have you experienced different levels of happiness and different periods of 'happiness' over time? If so, what factors do you think were making you more happy or less happy at different times?

2. Does 'happiness' mean the same thing to everybody?

Ask anyone, 'Would you like to be happier?' and the answer would surely be 'Yes, of course. Wouldn't we all?' Though perhaps some would respond, 'What do you mean by "happiness"?'

Some of us seek 'happiness' through greater wealth, some through better health, some through love and friendship, some through achievement, some through work, some through change, some through finding peace of mind and freedom from threat and problems.

'If you observe really happy people you will find them building a boat, writing a symphony, educating their children, growing double dahlias in their garden, or looking for dinosaur eggs in the Gobi desert. They will not be searching for happiness as if it were a button that has rolled under the radiator. They will not be striving for it as a goal in itself. They will have become aware that they are "happy" in the course of living life, twenty-four crowded hours of the day.'
Adapted from the psychiatrist W. Beran Wolfe

Possibly, for the two-thirds of the world who live in poverty, 'happiness' is just enough food and water to enable survival each day for themselves and their children.

introduction

What do you think has been, or is, the route to or the cause of most 'happiness' in your life? Has it always been like that or has it been different at different stages? Are you aware of people who seem to pursue happiness in different directions to you?

3. Is 'happiness' the purpose of life?

The purpose of life is a topic for endless debate. Why are we here? What is life all about? Does life have a purpose? If so, what is it? These are questions that lead to many philosophical, religious and pub discussions, produce many different opinions, but result in little consensus across a range of cultures. Whatever answers are suggested and whatever destinations are described, it is clear that much human energy is addressed to making our lives, our 'journeys', as happy as possible. If it is not our purpose to be 'happy' then certainly it is not our purpose to be *unhappy*, is it? Is our purpose to be richer, to be healthier, to achieve all we can, to have more pleasure, to love more, to make the world a better place, to live 'life to the full' (whatever that means to you), to make others happy, or what?

Tal Ben-Shahar[4] talks about the 'question of questions' which is: 'Why'? He says when we are asked, 'What do you want out of life?' or 'What do you want to achieve?' we should not be satisfied with our early answers. These might be the obvious answers such as 'wealth', 'a home with all the comforts', a 'beautiful, loving partner', a 'great job', 'promotion', 'good health', 'to win the lottery' and so on. Tal then says we should follow up with the question 'Why?' If that question 'Why?' continues to be repeated after each answer then eventually we will get to the ultimate answer which is we believe that if we get 'whatever', then the result is we will be 'happier'. All our intermediate aspirations, ambitions and desires are stepping stones to what we really want, which is to be 'happy'. It is surely a universally pursued goal. Being 'happier' is surely what most human beings spend most of their time and energy, most of their life, seeking to achieve.

---

4   Tal Ben-Shahar, Happier (McGraw-Hill, London, 2008).

introduction

Think about what you have 'searched' for in life so far and whether this has been, in fact, a stepping stone to being 'happier.' What is the goal you are currently pursuing and do you believe success will make you happy?

4. Is 'happiness' related to wealth?

There is no simple formula that says 'the richer you are the happier you are' or the 'poorer you are the more unhappy you will be'. The rich can be unhappy, the poor can be happy and vice versa. There is research that suggests that once we have 'enough' in terms of food, shelter, basic possessions and security then going on increasing our income will not necessarily make us 'happier'. The populations of wealthier Western countries do not report being as happy or as satisfied with their lives as were previous generations. There is evidence that increased materialism, where people attach more importance to money and possessions than to other life values (e.g. quality relationships, finding meaning, job satisfaction, etc.), does not produce greater happiness.

The philosopher A.C. Grayling[5] says:
' ... the man is poor who, despite owning millions, restlessly yearns for more because he feels he cannot have enough, and lacks the things money cannot buy. These unpurchasable treasures can never be left out of the picture: friendship, love, a sound digestion and a reliable, natural ability to sleep at nights. These are indispensable to the possibility of happiness, if not directly supplying it. The true equation between happiness and wealth is this: that happiness is wealth. Unlike wealth in the form of money and possessions, such happiness can never be quantified, only felt.'

---

5   A.C. Grayling is Professor of Philosophy at Birkbeck College, University of London <http://www.telegraph.co.uk/comment/3557112/Happiness-is-the-measure-of-true-wealth.html>.

introduction

This is not to say that there is no link between our level of income and our level of happiness. It is highly likely that if we become poorer after having had 'enough', then our level of 'happiness' would decrease.

Think about how you experience the link between your standard of living and your level of 'happiness'. Do you feel that having 'more' would increase it? How much is your level of 'happiness' based on what Grayling calls the 'unpurchasable treasures'?

5. Is 'happiness' just a modern fad?

There is evidence that the psychological and philosophical study and pursuit of 'happiness' began in China, India and Greece nearly 2,500 years ago with Confucius, Mencius, Buddha and Aristotle.[6] The ancient Greek philosopher Aristotle (384 BC–322 BC), a student of Plato and teacher of Alexander the Great, said:

'Happiness is the meaning and the purpose of life, the whole aim and end of human existence.'

In 1776 the American Declaration of Independence boldly claimed:

'We hold these truths to be self-evident, that all men are created equal, that they are endowed by their creator with certain unalienable rights, that among these are life, liberty and the pursuit of happiness.'

So, the subject has been around for some time and history suggests that the human species, since its very origins, put ever greater energy into seeking 'a better life' (i.e., a 'happier life'). Indeed, given the evidence of treasures buried with the wealthy of the ancient world, the search was for
a 'happier life' even beyond this one.

In recent decades the study of 'happiness' and its sources, has been taken up most valuably by the 'Positive Psychology' movement about which much more can be found on our website **www.livehappier.com**. So, the search for happiness is as old as human beings and as new as the twenty-first century!

---

[6] <http://www.pursuit-of-happiness.org/pursuit-of-happiness/history-of-happiness>.

 livehappier.com

introduction

Think about what you were taught about 'happiness' in life as you grew up. Were you taught it was what 'life was about'? Were you taught what it is and how you might achieve it?

what were you taught?

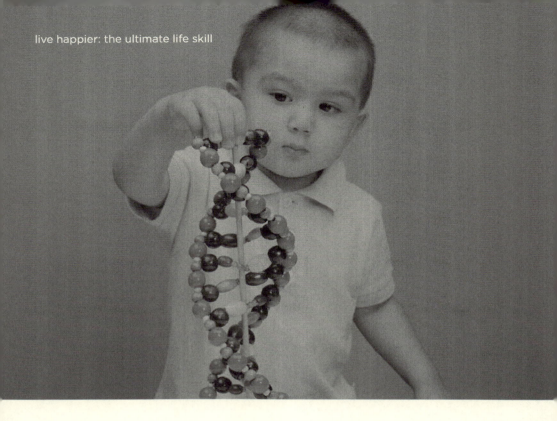

live happier: the ultimate life skill

6. Is 'happiness' genetic?

The work of Professor Timothy Bates suggests that about 50 per cent of our level of 'happiness' may be linked to our genes and our personality.[7] Personality traits such as 'sociable, active, stable, hardworking and conscientious' are more likely to produce lifestyles that lead to higher levels of 'happiness'. The interesting fact here is that if 50 per cent is 'given' and we are genetically inclined towards a particular general level of happiness, then there is still another 50 per cent which we can decide about, shape and influence.

A large research study by Professor Andrew Oswald[8] reported that whatever our individual personal happiness level there is a pattern to happiness over a lifetime. This pattern suggests that our lifetime happiness level is U-shaped – higher in our younger years, lowest in our mid-40s and higher again for 70 plus.

7 <http://www.time.com/time/printout/0,8816,1721954,00.html>.
8 David G. Blanchflower and Andrew J. Oswald, 'Is well-being U-shaped over the life cycle?', Social Science & Medicine, 66(8) (2008), 1733–49.

 livehappier.com

introduction

Think about what you know of your genetic history. Do you come from 'happier stock'? How does your own personality and 'happiness' level resemble those of your grandparents, parents, siblings and wider family? How much 'choice' do you feel you have to affect or influence your happiness level? Do you identify with the suggestion that happiness level is influenced by age?

write your thoughts here

7. Is 'happiness' all in the mind?

It is tempting to believe that our happiness is decided largely by external factors such as wealth, health, relationships, jobs and lifestyle options. Of course these are influential but perhaps even more significant is our 'internal' life. Sages old and new would offer the wisdom that 'happiness' is not drawn from what life brings us, but *from what we make of what life brings us*.

'Happiness' is not drawn from what life brings us, but from what we make of what life brings us!

Life brings pretty much the same challenges and events to most of us: birth, family life, relationships, education, work, change, loss, good times, hard times, ageing, health, plenty, shortage, reward, disappointment, celebration, crisis, decline, infirmity, death. Some people go through life and the experiences it brings reporting they have had a very happy life and others that life has been 'hell'. The differences are not about good fortune, plentiful resources, wealth or possessions. The differences seem to be about how we interpret and respond to our experiences.

Some survived the holocaust, others had years in unjust, cruel incarceration, some have great physical trauma, some great deprivation and still found that life was worth living. They viewed their suffering in a particular way and found meaning and worth beyond their pain and angst. Others endured what an outsider might see as 'less', saw their experience as mostly negative and regarded life as not worth living.

introduction

Think about your own view of 'happiness'. How much does it depend on 'external' factors? If so, what are they for you? How ready and able are you to respond robustly to the 'down times'? Do you search for any positive outcomes?

what are your views on happiness?

8. Is 'happiness' a political issue?

Politicians are becoming interested in what makes people happy because it is emerging that economic prosperity and the level of gross domestic product (GDP) are no longer delivering happiness. A poor economy is likely to make people unhappy; a growing economy is not in itself sufficient to make a population happy. Once we have 'enough', a home, food, clothes, security, then increased wealth does not seem to translate into greater happiness.

'Standards of living have increased dramatically and happiness has increased not at all, and in some cases has diminished slightly. There is a lot of evidence that being richer ... isn't making us happier.'
Professor Daniel Kahneman, University of Princeton

In 2006, an adviser to Tony Blair predicted that within 10 years the Government would be being judged not on how well the economy is doing but on how happy it is making people. A report[9] in that year said:

'Crippling depression and chronic anxiety are the biggest causes of misery in Britain today. They are the great submerged problem, which shame keeps out of sight. ... This is a waste of people's lives. It is also costing a lot of money. For depression and anxiety make it difficult or impossible to work, and drive people onto Benefits. We now have a million people on Incapacity Benefits because of mental illness – more than the total number of unemployed people receiving unemployment benefits

---

9 <http://cep.lse.ac.uk/textonly/research/mentalhealth/DEPRESSION_REPORT_LAYARD.pdf>.

... the total loss of output due to depression and chronic anxiety is some £12 billion a year – 1% of our total national income. Mental illness accounts for over a third of the burden of illness in Britain. ... Some 40% of all disability (physical and mental) is due to mental illness.'

That picture could be much worse today given the current economic crisis. Nobel prize-winning economists, Joseph E. Stiglitz and Amartya Sen, have been urging the politicians of the world to move beyond the simple measure of increased GDP as a country's achievements and begin to assess and report on their population's level of 'well-being'. In other words, progress should be measured in what the small nation of Bhutan has been pursuing since 1972, that is: GNH (gross national happiness). In 2009, President Sarkozy of France set up an advisory body including these two economists to advise his Government on how to move his country in that direction. In 2011, Prime Minister David Cameron created a similar initiative in the UK.

Positive Psychologists Ed Diener and Martin Seligman suggest measures of well-being (and 'happiness') would include the population's experience of 'engagement, purpose and meaning, optimism and trust, and positive and negative emotions in areas such as work life and social relationships.'

A.C. Grayling suggests:
'Instead of talking about happiness, one should talk about satisfaction, achievement, interest, engagement, enjoyment, growth and the constant opening of fresh possibilities.'

There's a challenge for the politicians of the future!

Think about your own view of 'happiness' and politics. Are the two linked at all? If so, what contributions do you think politicians can make to people's happiness and should governments be judged on how well they do this?

are happiness and politics linked?

9. Is 'happiness' just a myth or a mystery?

Most people would agree that 'happiness' exists. Hard as it is to define and achieve sometimes, we are all pretty sure it is 'out there somewhere' and well worth pursuing. Research into happiness usually starts by asking people to rate their own happiness levels. Questions such as 'Would you say you are very happy, happy, a little unhappy or very unhappy at the moment (or in life generally)?' can be answered without too much analysis or debate on the meaning of 'happiness'. Other questions about 'When have been your happiest and unhappiest times?' can again prompt ready answers. Happiness or its lack is experienced and talked about frequently on the understanding that we all know what it means and 'we have been there, done it, got the T-shirt' at some time or another.

What is also interesting is that research shows that our ratings of our own happiness levels can be supported or challenged by the observations of others who know us. When asked 'How would you rate how happy person X is?' the observer's answer often matches the happiness rating of the person themselves. So our 'happiness (or unhappiness) level' does come across to other people, our behaviour conveying what is going on inside. They may not know the causes but they do pick up the signals.

With ever increasing knowledge of how our brain works, neurologists are producing evidence of how scans can reveal the relationship between reported happiness and brain activity. Happiness has physiological dimensions.

live happier: the ultimate life skill

Think about how you would describe your own experience of happiness, and how real a part of your life it is or has been. How and why do you think it's important in life? Think of people you would regard as 'happy people.' What is the evidence? What are the 'signals' that make you say they are happy?

how to tell if someone is happy?

10. Is 'happiness' contagious or infectious?

Clearly, in a strictly physical sense, the answer is 'no'. However, 'happiness' research has established that we can 'live happier' by choosing to spend time with 'happier' people. Being in the company of people who are positive, optimistic, fun to be with, who are problem-solvers rather than problem-causers can affect our happiness levels. This does not mean simply being with people who have 'everything going for them' in terms of wealth, health and lifestyle. Rather, it means people of positive outlook, happy personality and demeanour. This does include people for whom life has its adversities but whose response to this is a positive outlook and real resilience. We can live 'happier' by being in the inspiring company of those who have met and do meet many challenges in life. We are social beings. The company of others does affect our moods and how we are affects them.

It is not just social interaction which can impact on our happiness level, but also the physical environment. Brooding, depressing, cold, dirty, threatening, dark circumstances can impact negatively on how we feel, especially if we spend appreciable time in such settings, and the opposite is true. Bright, warm, stimulating, colourful, energising environments can invite or support positive feelings and encourage well-being. We should choose our friends, our contacts, and our living and working space with happiness in mind.

live happier: the ultimate life skill

Think about how other people have impacted on your happiness levels for better or worse. Whose company has lifted your spirits, given you joy, encouraged achievement, made you laugh? How much time do you spend with such happiness inducers? Is it enough? How positive are the physical environments in which you live and work? How able are you to influence these?

who and what helps you to live happier?

11. Is 'happiness' just lots of pleasure?

Tal Ben-Shahar, in his excellent book 'Happier,'[10] distinguishes between pleasure and happiness and describes their relationship. Pleasure, he says, is the experience of positive feelings and:

'... is a pre-requisite for a fulfilling life ... The total absence of pleasure and the experience of constant emotional pain preclude the possibility of a happy life. When I speak of pleasure I am not referring to the experience of a constant 'high' or ecstasy. We all experience highs and lows. We can experience sadness at times ... and still lead a happy life ... Happiness does not require a constant experience of ecstasy, nor does it require an unbroken chain of positive emotions ... There is, then, more to happiness than positive emotions. ... Happiness is the overall experience of pleasure and meaning.'

Pleasure, he suggests, is the experience of feeling good in the here and now. Meaning comes from placing our experiences in a larger context, from having a sense of purpose, from seeing some benefit in the future from our actions, for working for that 'greater good'.

Mistaking pleasure for happiness can take us down some misleading avenues. Such a route can tempt us to believe simply that 'more means better'. Pleasure gained from alcohol, tobacco or narcotics can induce dependency and require increased doses to acquire the same effect. Excess and dependency are likely to greatly reduce our chances of living happier, as perhaps are pleasure pursuits that become obsessive or that marginalise those we care about.

---

10 Tal Ben-Shahar, Happier (McGraw-Hill, London, 2008).

The philosopher A.C. Grayling[11] warns against a simplistic view that pleasure equals happiness:

'If mere happiness were the point, we could easily achieve it for everyone by suitably medicating the water supply. But it has often been well said that the surest way to unhappiness is to seek happiness directly. Instead, happiness comes as a sideline of other endeavours that in themselves bring satisfaction and a sense of achievement.'

Professor Steven Reiss in an article 'Secrets of Happiness'[12] quotes the work of Harvard social psychologist William McDougall who maintained that people can be happy when in pain and unhappy when experiencing pleasure. The distinction is between 'feel-good' happiness and 'value-based' happiness. 'Feel-good' happiness is 'sensation-based' happiness (pursuing pleasures that give us kicks). It is short-lived and gets harder to replicate.

'Value-based' happiness is what we experience when our lives have meaning and purpose. It involves a 'spiritual source of satisfaction' that comes from living our deeper values. 'Value-based' happiness is the great leveller. We can achieve it whatever our status or condition in life. The poor can be as happy as the rich because true happiness comes from living in line with our values and finding meaning in life.

---

11 <http://www.telegraph.co.uk/comment/3557112/Happiness-is-the-measure-of-true-wealth.html>.
12 Steven Reiss, 'Secrets of Happiness', Psychology Today <http://psychologytoday.co./articles>. (The article goes on to offer the 'Reiss Profile' to help us identify 'The 16 Keys to Happiness'.)

introduction

Think about how you see the relationship between happiness and pleasure. How does one relate to the other in your life? What are the pleasures that are just that and what are the pleasures that relate to 'meaning'?

12. Can we learn to 'live happier'?

In President Obama's immortal assertion 'Yes we can!'

Though happiness as a pursuit is as ancient as human beings, the scientific world has only comparatively recently turned its attention to its study. Psychology made its mark in the Western world in the twentieth century through its focus and preoccupation with the study and treatment of mental illness. The factors that made people anxious, depressed, disturbed, neurotic and how they might be treated or healed was what intrigued most of the great minds of science. In 1998 psychologist Martin Seligman pointed out that the profession had spent many decades striving to get patients 'from -5 to zero' in terms of their mental well-being rather than, he suggested, 'from zero to +5'.

Psychology had been massively biased towards learning about 'malfunctioning' people and their struggles rather than asking what we can learn from the best performing, most successful, happiest of people. Seligman and colleagues of like mind formed the Positive Psychology[3] movement whose work would seek to reveal to the rest of us the components of lives that are achieving, creative, flourishing, fruitful, joyful, generous, virtuous, and examples of the highest achievements of human potential. The work of sociologist Aaron Antonovsky, based on his research into 'Salutogenesis' (the origins of health) was highly influential. He said let's study the highest functioning, healthiest individuals, groups, organisations, societies, populations. Let's learn from them and apply that learning to expand healthy living.

---

[11] The movement was and is built on and around the work of Abraham Maslow, Carl Rogers, Rollo May, Ed Diener, Martin Seligman, Aaron Antonovsky, Ellen Langer, Philip Stone, Tal Ben Shahar.

1.7 Life Skills for Living Happier in Eight Life Arenas

What follows is the opportunity to work with key findings from the research world of Positive Psychology. From the study of people, groups and organisations who have and are living effective, successful, flourishing lives, we can use that knowledge to assess our own approach to life, affirm the strengths we have and use our new awareness to add to what we have already. Those who get most from applying the evidence and wisdom there will be those who are open to a belief in lifelong learning, to an acceptance that our development is never over, to a readiness never to 'put a full stop' after ourselves, with an ambition to realise some more of the vast potential in each of us that goes untapped in one lifetime. Let us use the wisdom from the lives of so many others to expand our own capacity to 'live happier'!

Our quest for happier lives will invite you to review all eight of your life arenas, assessing the features of each in terms of its contribution to your general level of happiness, and being alert to how changes in some might enhance that level. A good metaphor for life is that it requires us to be an excellent 'plate spinner'. You will probably have seen jugglers set plates spinning on long bamboo canes, first one, then as it is spinning successfully another, and another, and so on until there might be a dozen spinning plates all kept up there by the juggler dashing backwards and forwards, re-tweaking any plate that looks to be falling. So, it can feel for us that we have to attend to the arenas of our life with similar skill, alertness and zeal to be able to live happier.

This book will focus on the life skills for living happier in the eight major arenas of life: **relationships, work, money, health, leisure, learning, home and spirituality.**

live happier: the ultimate life skill

So, how happy are you?

Here's an easy and visual way to get a snapshot of how happy you are, and so where you might best focus your efforts in order to feel happier. Simply rate yourself (5 being the happiest) on each axis with a small dot, then join the dots up afterwards - you'll quickly see where the gaps are. Consider repeating this exercise over time.

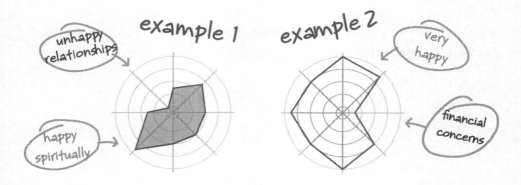

livehappier.com

introduction

In addition, the website (www.livehappier.com) will focus on some generic life skills that are likely to make us more successful and happy in 'juggling' our life. These skills have huge value in life generally and equip us to be effective and achieve more in every arena. These skills are numerous, generic and applicable to the whole of our lives. They are indeed life skills for living happier and we will be offering them to you as we expand the website.

'I believe life is constantly testing us for our level of commitment and life's greatest rewards are reserved for those who demonstrate a never-ending commitment to act until they achieve. This level of resolve can move mountains, but it must be constant and consistent. As simplistic as this may sound, it is still the common denominator separating those who live their dreams from those who live with regret.'
Anthony Robbins, Life Coach

live happier: the ultimate life skill

relationships

quality relationships

This chapter addresses the key area of relationships and 'living happier'.

 livehappier.com

Relationships and Happiness

This chapter addresses the key area of relationships and 'living happier'. It introduces research that shows that quality relationships are at the core of happier living. It will:

- invite you to reflect on which relationships have been and are the source of greatest happiness in your life so far and what you can learn from them about how to 'live happier' now and in the future;
- introduce the concept of 'supportive' relationships and their contribution to happier living;
- inform you what research tells us about the nature and value of friendships;
- share the latest research on the potential of friendships at work to contribute to life satisfaction and well-being.

As with all the chapters in this book, the information it provides will offer the opportunity to enhance relationships in your life.

To achieve this will require the application to your life of the evidence and advice it offers. Having information is in itself not sufficient to achieve change. Change requires motivation, hard work and persistence, but 'living happier' is worth that effort.

What is Known About Relationships and Happiness?

Positive Psychology research shows us that, after a certain level of economic well-being, it isn't money, material, physical pleasures, or increased possessions that help us to live happier. The key ingredients are:

- **Positive Relationships:**[1] having strong, deep and wide, quality relationships, the deeper and wider the better;
- **Meaning in Life:** having a belief in and involvement with something 'bigger than ourselves', which may be a religion, spirituality, a worthy cause or a strong philosophy of life; and
- **Goals in Life:** that are aligned with our values that lead us to do enjoyable, interesting work and be involved in activities using our strengths and skills.

In their excellent book[2] 'Happiness – Unlocking the Mysteries of Psychological Wealth', Professor Ed Diener and his son Robert pose us an artificial, but interesting, possibility;

Invaders, extremely advanced aliens, arrive to carry out an experiment on Planet Earth. They remove every other human being on the planet and leave just us, with the whole planet at our disposal. Our safety is guaranteed; food, drink, transport, indeed all resources are endlessly available to us and we can live as long as we want – our only lack will be the company of any other human being. The aliens retire to observe our response.

---

1 Professor Ed Diener as reported in <http://news.bbc.co.uk/player/nol/newsid_4810000/newsid_4812700/4812742.stm?bw=bb&mp=wm&news=1>.
2 Ed Diener and Robert Biswas-Diener, Happiness – Unlocking the Mysteries of Psychological Wealth (Blackwell, 2008).

relationships and happiness

How Would We React?

The Dieners speculate that many of us would head off initially into a period of hedonistic consumption and enjoyment. The best food and drink, wonderful properties, first class travel, the most beautiful resorts, the best jewellery, art, technology and all aspects of luxury living endlessly available – just nobody else to share them with! There is a one-liner that says 'hell is other people'. But what would life be like with no other human contact?

What Would We Miss?

We would have an endless supply of all material luxuries, but the Dieners query how much happiness we would experience if we have no one with whom to share our life and its pleasures. There would be no partners in enjoyment with whom to converse, have a drink or meal, share how we feel, discuss what's in the media, convey how beautiful we find the sunsets or the night skies, laugh, play games.

There would be no one to help us or for us to help, no children to cuddle, no one to care for or be cared for by, no one to love or to love us. How long would we want to live like that?

It would be a life of solitary confinement, in luxury circumstances it's true, but surely offering only endless loneliness, frustration and despair that all the possessions in the world could not compensate for. We are essentially social creatures wired for relationships, for companionship, for interaction, for cooperation, for competition, for love and being loved, and the experience of satisfying or otherwise those needs in ourselves will surely decide how happily we live.

What are 'They' Worth?

And the evidence is that it is not just our closest relationships that we value.

Getting on well with the folks next door could be worth the equivalent of earning an extra £40,000 per year. Maybe you are muttering, 'you don't know my neighbours!' Researchers[1] asked people to put a monetary value on certain relationships and other factors in their life, as compared with potential pay increases they might receive instead, i.e., what would it be worth to you per annum to have X?

Based on this theoretical trade-off, the answers suggested that we would value:

- good health as being worth the equivalent of £251,000 a year;
- excellent health as being worth the equivalent of £304,000 a year;
- marriage as being worth the equivalent of £53,833 a year;
- living together as being worth the equivalent of £82,500 a year (sic) more highly valued than marriage!;
- separation as being worth minus the equivalent of £57,667 a year (the separated had the lowest levels of life satisfaction);
- divorce as being worth minus the equivalent of £24,500 a year;
- being widowed as being minus the equivalent of £200,000 a year (the loss of a spouse has one of the biggest negative effects on health and happiness);

what would it be worth to you?

---

[1] Article by Roger Dobson in The Times, June 2007 based on Dr Nattavudh Powdthavee, 'Putting a Price Tag on Friends, Relatives and Neighbours', Journal of Social Economics, April 2007 <http://www.unisi.it/eventi/happiness/curriculum/nattavudh.pdf>.

- meeting good friends and close relatives:
  - 'once or twice a month' worth the equivalent of £35,000 a year;
  - 'once or twice a week' worth the equivalent of £50,500 a year;
  - 'most days' worth the equivalent of £63,833 a year.

Author and Psychology Professor Ed Diener,[2]

'It is important to work on social skills, close interpersonal ties and social support in order to be happy.'

Relationships – the Core of Happier Living

So, while work, wealth, health, learning and pleasure might matter a great deal to us, it is likely to be the relationships in our lives that have most to do with our happiness and life satisfaction. Indeed, across the whole of our lives, our mental and physical health, our longevity, and our all round well-being and life satisfaction will be greatly linked to the extent and quality of the relationships we have. Because we are social animals, we cannot live healthily or happily in isolation. Those we interact with are an essential part of our life and our happiness and potentially they will be very major contributors to them. We have only to consider the vast number of human interactions that take place each day, face-to-face, and via technology. Reflect on the ubiquitous mobile phone, on the amount of participation in social networking sites such as Facebook, You Tube and Twitter, on the mountain of emails and even snail mail, and recognise that relationships are central to our lives, and to our happiness or otherwise.

2 Claudia Wallis, 'The New Science of Happiness', Time Magazine, 9 January 2005 <http://www.time.com/time/magazine/article/0,9171,1015902,00.html>.

> 'You can kiss your family and friends good-bye and put miles between you, but at the same time you carry them with you in your heart, your mind, your stomach, because you do not just live in a world, but a world lives in you.'
> Frederick Buechner, Theologian

Activity 1: Relationships – Starting Point

Happiness is a virtuous cycle. Positive relationships mean we live happier, and happier people create more positive relationships. The Dieners offer a short but valuable checklist on our personal style and social skills by asking us to reflect on 10 statements and answer 'yes' or 'no' to each, depending on whether we think each one is true of ourselves or not. (The following list is adapted from their version.)

My Starting Point

Put a **3** against the statements that are true of you and an **X** against those that are not.

> I am positive in how I relate to people, regularly paying compliments and speaking and acting positively.
>
> I have a very close relationship with someone with whom I can share my most intimate thoughts and feelings.
>
> I am rarely, if ever, lonely.

relationships and happiness

I rarely, if ever, speak negatively to or about others.

My relationships with colleagues are very positive.

I have friends that I relax and feel at ease with.

I trust my family and friends.

There are people I love and care about and who love and care about me.

I have people I can always contact in an emergency.

There are people I can have great fun with.

The suggestion is that if we can tick between 8 and 10 of those questions then our social well-being is likely to be on very firm foundations and we will be well on the way to 'living happier'.

Complete these sentences:

This checklist tells me that my starting point in relating to other people is:

Very positive _____

Fairly positive _____

Could be more positive _____

_____

To make it even more positive I could:

_____

_____

_____

_____

'Having someone wonder when you don't come home at night is a very old human need.'
Margaret Mead, Anthropologist

relationships and happiness

Activity 2: Relationships and Happiness in My Life So Far

Here is a breakdown of the stages of your life so far in periods of 15 years. Reflect on each period relevant to your life so far and write or type in which relationships brought you most happiness in that period and what that taught you about relationships and happiness. For example, my Granny – warmth and kindness, taught me that making other people happy really matters, etc.

0-15 years (think parents, step parents, foster or adoptive parents, guardians, brothers, sisters, step brothers and sisters, extended family, teachers, friends, neighbours, econtacts on social media, etc.)

16-30 years (think family, children, friends, extended family, teachers, neighbours, managers, workmates, partners, econtacts on social media, etc.)

31-45 years (think partners, family, children, grandchildren, friends, extended family, managers, colleagues, neighbours and contacts on social media etc.)

46-60 (think as above)

61-75 (think as above)

relationships and happiness

Over 75 (think as above)

_____

_____

Reflecting on your history of relationships, summarise here on what are the most important lessons in life about relationships and happiness for you so far.

_____

_____

_____

Complete the sentence:

What my life so far has taught me about relationships and happiness is:

_____

_____

_____

live happier: the ultimate life skill

'Thousands of candles can be lighted from a single candle and the life of a candle will not be shortened. Happiness never decreases by being shared.'
Buddha

relationships and happiness

Activity 3: Relationships and Happiness in My Life Now

Think some more about how much relationships contribute to happiness in your life right now.

Score each relationship listed, as follows:
1 = Not a source of happiness for me.
2 = Source of some happiness for me.
3 = Source of significant happiness for me.
4 = Source of great happiness for me.

Ignore any relationship listed which does not exist for you.

My Family Relationships

My relationship with my parents, step, foster or adoptive parents, guardians	
My relationship with my brothers/sisters/step, foster or adoptive brothers/sisters	
My relationship with my grandparents, step, foster or adoptive grandparents, guardians	

My relationship with my wider family/foster or adoptive family (aunts, uncles, cousins, etc.)	
My relationship with my spouse/partner	
My relationship with my children	
My relationship with my grandchildren	
TOTAL	

My Work Relationships

My relationship with my peers	
My relationship with my supervisor/manager	
My relationship with those I supervise/manage	
My relationship with my customers/those I provide a service to	
TOTAL	

relationships and happiness

My Social Relationships

My partner

My close friends

My network of acquaintances/wider social contacts

My social network contacts

My neighbours

People in the communities/clubs/teams/groups I belong to

TOTAL

Totals

My Family Relationships

My Work Relationships

My Social Relationships

What do the scores on page 63 tell you about relationships as a source of happiness in your life? (Put a 3 against the answer you think is most true for you.)

Balanced: I have a good range of relationships which are positive and help me to live happier

Not balanced enough: I may be relying too much on one area of relationships and missing out on others

Work to be done: I could be happier if I worked on a particular area of relationships

Complete this sentence:

These are the relationships that help me live happier:

_____

_____

_____

relationships and happiness

These are the relationships which make me less happy:
_____
_____
_____

I would like to strengthen my relationship with:
_____
_____
_____

What would I most want to change, if anything, about any of these relationships?
_____
_____
_____

complete this

'**Psychological wealth is your true total net worth, and includes your attitudes towards life, social support, spiritual development, material resources, health, and activities in which you engage.**'
Ed Diener, Author and Psychology Professor

relationships and happiness

Activity 4: Who Do I Help to Live Happier?

Reflecting further, let's not think only of the happiness or otherwise that we receive from our relationships, but also (as all happy relationships are win-win) let's ask ourselves how much happiness we believe we give to others.

Complete these sentences:

I believe I make the following people happier in my relationships with them:

_____
_____
_____

I would like to make the following people happier in my relationships with them:

_____
_____
_____

complete these

live happier: the ultimate life skill

What I could I do to achieve this is:

So, you have begun to focus on some of the links in your life between relationships and happiness. Let us take this further by working on some life skills that are essential for happier relationships.

relationships and happiness

Life Skill: Build Quality Relationships

Just 'wanting' quality relationships in itself is not enough. People can't read our minds. The majority do 'read' the way we behave and are attracted or put off by that. Even when we are not speaking we are communicating through our body language and there is some evidence that this can 'speak' even louder than words. By increasing our awareness of the 'behaviours' that research tells us can build happier, more positive, longer lasting, health-building relationships, we can enhance our ability to deepen and increase our most important relationships.

Activity 5: Making Relationships Work

A very significant twentieth-century psychologist Carl Rogers[1] established through his work that:
- as healthy human beings we are ambitious to become all we are capable of becoming;
- we are always aspiring to be more than we are, to realise all the potential we have;
- we are social beings and are affected by and constantly interact with those around us for better or for worse;
- healthy, happy living results from having a sense of our own worth (having positive self-esteem; not believing that we are perfect, but believing that we are worthwhile and significant).

Relationships that recognise our worth and the worth of others are the basis for healthy, flourishing lives.

What Counts the Most?

Rogers recognised three features of relationships that produce health and well-being for those involved in them. The language used to define the three features varies, but essentially Rogers was saying that quality relationships are built upon:
- **Respect:** when we behave towards another person in ways that 'say' to them that they are valued, significant and worthwhile;
- **Understanding:** when we show other people that we can understand 'how they see and feel about things'; that we can see their perspective and point of view; that we can see things their way and not just our own;

---

1   <http://en.wikipedia.org/wiki/Carl_Rogers>.

- **Genuineness:** when relationships are based on openness, honesty, trustworthiness; without deceit or 'mixed messages'.

A person's uniqueness, dignity and worth are what bring out the best in human beings. These are needs in life that are central to living happier lives. Rogers did not 'invent' those features. His research found that these were the qualities evident in healthy, positive, flourishing relationships. If we receive them we grow, and we will live happier lives. If we lack them we are likely to struggle. If we relate in these ways towards other people they will grow healthily and live happier from that experience.

It's All About Behaviour

It is important to note that 'behaviours' are at the heart of human interaction and are the 'stuff' of relationships. We cannot read each other's minds (maybe thankfully). We just 'read' the way people behave towards us and vice versa. We hang on to 'words' because they seem to be massively important, but the evidence is that 'non-verbal' behaviours are even more persuasive.

Some estimates suggest that up to 90 per cent of communication between people can be in non-verbal signals; in our tone of voice, the expression on our face, the look in our eyes, our 'body language'. We might say 'I really like you', but if we look cross or bored or distracted or preoccupied as we say it we are unlikely to be believed. We are always communicating whether we realise it or not. What messages are we giving out?

Some people seem to be more successful in building relationships than others. Often, such people seem to be more naturally attractive, more outgoing, easier to be with, 'warmer', more 'sociable'. These are all words to describe people who behave in particular ways. Their attractiveness may seem somehow magical, mystical or natural to those of us less adept at attracting others, but, in fact, they have learned (maybe subconsciously) in their upbringing what it takes to 'get on' with other people.

Think of the best relationships in your life, the people you are closest to, and have them in mind as you work through the following list of statements other people have made about what makes them like their friends or closest relations. Tick the ones you agree with.

The people I am closest to:

'Show they like me, take an interest in me, don't always go on about their own stuff. Being with them makes me feel good.'

'Listen to me. They see my point of view.'

'Are reliable. I can always depend on them. They don't let me down.'

'Want to spend time with me and make time for that.'

'Are good fun. We can let our hair down and laugh a lot together.'

'Are loyal. They don't go off me if I get something wrong. They are forgiving.'

'Go out of their way for me. Take trouble to please me.'

'Are interested in the things I am interested in.'

relationships and happiness

'We like similar things.'

'Don't cause me problems. They care about me.'

'Are generous. It's never all take and no give!'

'Enable me to be myself with them. I'm free to be me!'

'Give me space and time. They are hassle free.'

'Are people it's easy to be with. I know where I am with them, no issues.'

'Are people where what you see is what you get. Nothing two-faced, nothing "behind your back". I can always trust them.'

What would you have added about the things those you are closest to do or don't do that makes them attractive to you?

_____
_____
_____
_____

> What do you think it is that you do or don't do that makes you attractive to them?
>
> _____
>
> _____
>
> _____
>
> Check out your answers with them at some point if that is appropriate.

You might have mentioned 'good looks' and 'pots of money' because those can be the initial, flip responses. However, beyond those more superficial things we are attracted to people who:
- make us feel good about ourselves;
- make us feel worthwhile;
- we can depend on and trust; and
- seem to understand and appreciate our unique 'take' on the world.

Unless those deeper 'messages' are present for real in a relationship then the 'looks and money' may not be enough.

relationships and happiness

What Rogers was telling us was that quality relationships are built on:
- the way we behave towards each other in ways that make each of us feel special;
- a mutual exchange of attraction and trust and are essential to a healthy, happy life.

Think about the following:

Which are the relationships that are most special and important at this stage in your life?

___

___

___

What do other people do that makes you feel valued, worthwhile or special?

___

___

___

What can you continue to do, or do more often, to make those you care most about feel even more special, appreciated and understood?
_____
_____

Which are the relationships that matter to you that you might need to give more attention to?
_____
_____

What would you need to do to strengthen or repair those? Do you want to do that?
_____
_____

relationships and happiness

Life Skill: Build Supportive Relationships

'If I am not for myself, who will be for me? If I am only for myself, what am I? And if not now, when?'
The Talmud (Central text of mainstream Judaism)

Good and plentiful social relationships are essential to our well-being and happiness. In the evolution of human beings much has been gained from living cooperatively. Living in groups has provided us with so much in terms of survival and growth: mutual protection, practical help, shared learning, joint problem-solving, expanded support, language and skill development, cultural enjoyment, community participation and much, much more. Contacts with and support from a wide social network are central to life and to living happier.

'The quantity and quality of our social relationships strongly affects our health. People with larger social support networks and stronger social bonds with members of their networks have better physical and mental health, fewer illnesses and less depression, recover more rapidly from physical illness and psychological problems and have a lower risk of death.'
Shelle E Taylor, Psychology Professor[1]

Our social network and the relationships it makes possible answer a deep psychological need, a need that if unanswered can produce loneliness and a lack of meaning and unhappiness.

That need is to 'belong,'[2] to be accepted, to be approved of, to be admired and valued, to be part of something that is more than just ourselves; the need for relationships, the need for connection and engagement, the need for support.

'Happier people do more frequent altruistic acts ... spend a greater percentage of their time helping others ... and (at work are more likely to) go beyond the call of duty!'
Sonja Lyubormirsky, Psychologist

---

1   Taylor et al., 'Toward a Biology of Social Support' in C.R. Snyder and Shane J. Lopez (eds.) Handbook of Positive Psychology (Oxford University Press, New York, 2002).
2   R.F. Baumeister and M.R. Leary, 'The need to belong: Desire for interpersonal attachments as a fundamental human motivation', Psychological Bulletin, 117 (1995), 497–529.

relationships and happiness

Where Do I Find Support?

Our evolutionary history has produced communities which today offer extraordinary levels of support, levels that would have seemed incredible to our ancestors. People all over the world produce the food we eat and goods we need. At home, people run schools that educate our children, provide doctors to heal our sicknesses, offer emergency services that rescue and defend us, make laws that protect our rights, run agencies that produce and supply energy to our homes, clean water through our taps, and remove and dispose of our waste.

An impressive support system indeed, but one that supplies all we need to 'live happier'? No!

What we need to 'live happier' goes beyond all the above. We are hardwired with a need for human, interpersonal, psychological, social and emotional support. People with high levels of social support:

- are more extrovert and less neurotic;
- are less stressed and cope better with life and its challenges;
- attract help readily and willingly from their social network;
- have much more social support, though they need it less.

Look at the different kinds of support that people have suggested they value on pages 80-84. Enter the names of people you know who can or do provide that type of support for you. Leave blank any type of support you feel you don't have.

Activity 6: Types of Support

1. Someone who listens to me, someone I can talk things through with and 'get things off my chest'.

   For me this is _____

2. Someone I can let off steam with, let my hair down with.

   For me this is _____

3. Someone I can relax with, chill out with.

   For me this is _____

4. Someone wise and knowledgeable I can turn to for advice.

   For me this is _____

5. Someone I can talk through problems with and confide in.

   For me this is _____

who are they?

relationships and happiness

6. Someone who knows how to get things done, who is practical and experienced.

   For me this is _____

7. Someone I can talk to about my feelings (e.g. anger, worry, fear, love, etc.)

   For me this is _____

8. Someone who can give me feedback on myself, tell me what they think about me.

   For me this is _____

9. Someone who likes culture. Someone I can go with to the theatre, cinema or a concert.

   For me this is _____

10. Someone I can call on in a crisis.

    For me this is _____

11. Someone who introduces me to new ideas, new interests, new people.

    For me this is _____

12. Someone to have a really good laugh with.

    For me this is _____

13. Someone to share really good news with.

    For me this is _____

14. Someone who challenges me to sit up and take a good look at myself.

    For me this is _____

15. Someone who can give me practical or material support.

    For me this is _____

relationships and happiness

16. Someone who is a specialist in my field that I can swap ideas with.

    For me this is _____

17. Someone who can make me feel competent and valued.

    For me this is _____

18. Someone who will support and encourage me through changes I want to make.

    For me this is _____

19. Someone whose company makes me feel energised and revived.

    For me this is _____

20. Someone, who has expertise in areas I need help with (e.g. technology, finance, the family, DIY, children, the law, etc.)

For me this is _____

Where are the gaps? Fill in here any kind of support you would like or need that is not mentioned above.

_____
_____
_____

All the people you have named above are part of your support network. How many names are in your network? The more names, the stronger your network! Is your network big enough, strong enough?

relationships and happiness

Avoiding 'All Our Eggs in One Basket'

A frequent result of reflections like this is that we find that many of our support needs are met by us having 'all our eggs in one basket'. Most commonly, a partner has to bear the whole brunt of supporting us. They not only provide for most of our emotional, physical and psychological needs, but they often have to 'pick up the pieces' in the evening if we have had a hard day, or sit and watch us in a couch potato or zombie state.

Expecting a partner or one person to provide all our support needs:
- is likely to be very unfair and even stressful to them;
- means we could be missing out on other expertise;
- is high risk because they may not always be there or may find our demands too great.

This may need explaining to a partner because if they care for us they will want to be everything to us. Caring for them might mean us not expecting them to take on the whole task of providing for all our various support needs. And, of course, vice versa. Discuss it with them if that would be useful..

The healthiest and most valuable support systems have breadth and depth. They are multifaceted, diverse, willing and able. We should therefore try to ensure we have a deep and wide support network with a range of skills and experience.

Activity 7: Extending Our Network

What if our network is not extensive enough? We then may need to meet more people and find more people that we feel compatible with, who share our interests, who we get on well with. We can't do this by staying at home.

How to make our network bigger
Which of the following activities could help you extend your network so that you can get to know more people and make more contacts?

Put a tick against the ones that appeal to you.

Join a gym

Work as a volunteer

Join a neighbourhood or residents' group

Join a walking/athletic/sports group

Set up a facebook page

Join a knitting circle

Join a debating society

Meet other parents through a crèche or school pta

Sign up for an adult education course

Become a friend of a theatre

Take up a sport as a player or supporter

Start a linkedin group

tick the boxes

relationships and happiness

Take Up A Cause, Get Involved In Local Politics ☐

Join A Religious Community ☐

Accept Social Invitations To Things Like parties, Social Or Fundraising Events ☐

Join In Pub Quiz Nights ☐

Start A Blog ☐

Join A Choir ☐

Invite People Round For A Meal ☐

Say 'Yes' To Work's Nights Out ☐

Join A Gardening/Allotment Club ☐

Join A Dance Class Or A Swimming Club ☐

Join A Book Or Hobby Club ☐

These are just some of the options. What others would you recommend?

_____
_____
_____
_____

tick the boxes

Making it Happen

What these options provide are opportunities. They can put us in a context in which we can meet people, some of whom could well become valuable members of our support network. It is useful to remember that building relationships takes time and skills. We can build a range of relationships with different 'levels' and importance.

Level 1 – our relationships at this initial level are on the surface; we exchange factual information with somebody as we get to know each other where we live and/or work, holidays we've taken, films/shows we've seen, our hobbies, our family, contacts or friends on Facebook, Twitter etc, basic contacts, exchanging factual, information about ourselves.

Write in the names of two people you have a relationship with at this level

_____

_____

Level 2 – we begin to exchange opinions which can take us deeper and closer to somebody; we talk about shows, films, books that we liked or disliked, what we think about events in the news; opinions are riskier than facts so they can take us closer (if they are shared by the other person) or begin a drift away (if the other disagrees).

Write in the names of two people you have a relationship with at this level

_____

_____

write two names

relationships and happiness

Level 3 – with some people our relationship goes deeper; now we begin to tell about our feelings; here we may talk about hopes and anxieties, what makes us happy or angry, what we feel passionate about; talking about feelings is riskier again, we are revealing things about ourselves that might bring us closer (if the other person responds in the same way) or separate us (if the other person becomes uneasy about what we are saying). Deeper relationships do require us to take more of a risk.

> Write in the names of two people you have a relationship with at this level.
>
> _____
>
> _____

Level 4 – with time and the development of trust we can become very close to some people, a few special ones; with them we can each communicate about ourselves at an intimate level and if trust is built we will have very special relationships with them. This level needs skill and care and risk, but it is where we may find our soul mates, our true and priceless friendships and supports, and it is likely to be where we find the most rewarding relationships of our life.

> Write in the names of two people you have a relationship with at this level.
>
> _____
>
> _____

write two names

live happier: the ultimate life skill

'Perhaps the most important reason for self-disclosure is that without it we cannot truly love.'
Sidney Jourard,
The Transparent Self

relationships and happiness

Widening Our Networks

What do you think are the best, most appealing ways in which you could increase your social network if you wished to?

Remember that seeking support is a sign of strength. Too many of us lack the courage to ask, or see having to ask for help as a weakness.

Part of the 'live happier' future is the development of a worldwide virtual community through the website, through which we can share our thoughts, ideas and experiences, and build an even wider social network for ourselves.

Hear the Expert

Hear a fascinating account by Nicholas Christakis of research into social networks.[8]
Joint author (with James Fowler) of a most original book titled 'Connected: The Surprising Power of Our Social Networks and How They Shape Our Lives', Nicholas reveals to us how the networks we are part of can influence whether we are happy, sad, obese, healthy, and so much more.

---

8   <http://connectedthebook.com/pages/authors.html>.
    <http://www.ted.com/talks/nicholas_christakis_the_hidden_influence_of_social_networks.html>.

On the basis of your reflections on Relationships and Happiness so far, and the information you have worked with in this chapter, write in what you would like more of, less of and what you would like to keep the same in your life right now. Reflect on your relationships and identify changes you would like to make.

More of	Less of	Keep the same

relationships and happiness

Choose three things that you would like to start working on as a priority.

1.

2.

3.

You may wish to take the key topic of Relationships further on the Live Happier website (www.livehappier.com) where you can find the following life skills:

- **Create Deep and Lasting Intimate Relationships**
- **Have Friends at Work**
- **Create Positive Family Relationships**
- **Form Strong Friendships**
- **Use Social Media to Help You Live Happier.**

live happier: the ultimate life skill

work

let's be clearer about 'work'

Do you work? Of course you do. We all do.
So why do some people say they don't?

 livehappier.com

Work and Happiness

Because we still live with an outdated concept of work that equates it with employment, work for many still means having a paid job.

We want to challenge that simplistic link, believing it can block a more creative way of looking at our work and our life. Let's be clearer as to what 'work' is.

Activity 1: What is Work?

- It is an activity.
- It can provide us with a sense of purpose and direction.
- It can provide a structure for our life.
- It can be where we learn and develop new skills.
- It can give us an identity and self-respect.
- It can provide us with friends and a community.
- It can influence how other people see and feel about us.

Oh yes, and it can provide us with money if somebody wants to buy what our work produces.

Seth Godin's succinct blog postings are always worth looking at: www.sethgodin.com. He has his own suggestions as to the reasons why we work. He says we work:

1. For the money.
2. To be challenged.
3. For the pleasure/calling of doing the work.
4. For the impact it makes on the world.
5. For the reputation we build in the community.
6. To solve interesting problems.
7. To be part of a group and to experience the mission.
8. To be appreciated.

He then asks why the focus is always on the first. Why do we advertise jobs or promotions and just emphasise the wage or salary? Good question Seth.

Ask yourself this question: how would you rank order these eight statements in terms of what you look for in work? Write your rankings in the boxes provided.

work and happiness

Has doing the ranking helped you realise more about your own reasons for working? How much is it about 'more than the money' for you? Write in your views.

'And What Do You Do?'

How do you answer that question at social gatherings? Those who work tend to introduce themselves in terms of their occupation as this provides an easy topic to begin a conversation. It is fairly common for people who have no paid work to explain, almost apologetically, 'I'm retired', or 'I'm only a housewife', or 'I'm unemployed'. Some who have no paid work have said, 'It is as if in some people's eyes and more importantly in our own eyes we have suddenly become invisible.'

The relationship between 'work' and 'worth' is so powerful that when paid work is not part of our lives we can feel less valuable to ourselves, to our family, to our friends and to the wider society. This is the thinking we need to challenge.

There may sometimes be a shortage of jobs but there will never be a shortage of work!

A teacher becoming unemployed will still have those teaching skills and will still be capable of using them in a wide variety of situations. The same is true of a salesperson, an electrician, a car mechanic, librarian, IT worker, customer service agent, carer, etc.

The distinction between paid and unpaid work, and the implications of the different attitudes to each one, is crucial at all stages in our lives. We all need work. Without it we might just psychologically wither, but we can do work that is valuable and has meaning even if it is not paid work.

What is Known About Work and Happiness?

The research[1] tells us that the happiest people at work:
- get promoted faster;
- earn more;
- get more support;
- generate better and more creative ideas;
- achieve goals faster;
- interact better with colleagues and bosses;
- receive better reviews;
- learn more;
- achieve greater success;
- are healthier.

---

1 Jessica Pryce-Jones, Happiness at Work: Maximising your Psychological Capital for Success (Wiley-Blackwell, 2010). More research detailed in Peter Warr, Work, Happiness, and Unhappiness (Lawrence Erlbaum Associates, 2007).

In addition, employers like happy workers as they:
- are almost 50 per cent more productive (they contribute nearly 1.25 days a week more than their less happy colleagues);
- take only 1.5 days a year off sick compared with the average of six days in the private sector and up to 20 days in the public sector;
- have 180 per cent more energy;
- are 155 per cent happier than the least happy workers;
- are 108 per cent more engaged in their work;
- report 82 per cent more job satisfaction;
- are 50 per cent more motivated;
- feel they achieve their potential 40 per cent more than unhappy workers;
- get 28 per cent more respect from colleagues and 31 per cent more from their bosses;
- are 25 per cent more effective;
- have 25 per cent more self-belief.

Activity 2: How Happy are You at Work?

You are likely to spend between 75,000 and 100,000 hours in paid work in your lifetime. So, how happy are you with your work right now?

Any job we choose to do will probably have elements of it that we love and also have 'grunt work' as part of it. 'Grunt work' is what you would really not choose to do but you have to do it as it's part of the job. The hope is that the 'grunt' part never takes up more than 20 per cent of our time. Sadly we all know people where that percentage is easily exceeded.

Think of the job or jobs you currently do. Also, think of a job you might be interested in pursuing.

Write in the job titles below then write in what you think is the grunt work percentage of that job and what you think is the 'work you love' percentage. There will probably also be a percentage that is at neither extreme that we can call 'mundane work'.

Job 1 Title _____

% Grunt work _____ Mundane work _____ Work you love _____

Job 2 Title _____

% Grunt work _____ Mundane work _____ Work you love _____

Job 3 Title _____

% Grunt work _____ Mundane work _____ Work you love _____

So what does this tell you about your work right now?

If you are doing far too much grunt work and mundane work, then you might well want to work on some of the life skills for living happier that follow.

You will live happier at work if you:
- find meaningful paid or unpaid work;
- use your motivated skills;
- ensure that your work matches your values.

When thinking about work we always need to start by being clear what we really want to achieve through it – what are our goals, our purpose, what is meaningful to us.

From there we can focus on the skills we want to use to achieve these things. We call these motivated skills – those skills that we are born to use and that we love to exercise.

But to live happier in our work we need to be clear that our goals and purpose are truly things we value and that the route we take to achieve them is very much aligned with our underlying values.

The following life skills will help us achieve all of these.

live happier: the ultimate life skill

Life Skill: Discover Our Motivated Skills

'What a person is good at or not is a given. A person's way of performing can be slightly modified but it is unlikely to be completely changed – and certainly not easily.'
Peter Drucker, Management expert

We all have things we love to do: making things, drawing them, designing them, inventing them, building them, solving problems, writing, persuading, helping people, teaching, mentoring, networking… you get the idea.

work and happiness

We feel most alive when we do 'things' that we love to do and conversely we feel pretty miserable when we don't. Those 'things' are actually the skills that we were born to use – that we're 'motivated' to use. A motivated skill is linked to our temperament and is something we are born with. It dictates how we prefer to behave.

Bernard Haldane was the first career development specialist to suggest we learn best from our successes and not our failures. He developed the concept of 'motivated skills' after moving to the US from England after the Second World War. He worked with thousands of returning US service people and developed his approach from this experience as he was appalled to discover just how few people had any idea of what skills they had and what skills they wanted to use.

He discovered that it was possible to identify what, by then, he was calling 'motivated skills' at an early age. A four-year-old who enjoys performing will enjoy it at 15 or 20 or 80 – unless discouraged from doing so. A seven-year-old who's sensitive and likes to help people is also likely to want to do that throughout his or her life.

Conversely, those who show no talent for constructing or building things early on are unlikely to ever love that activity, no matter how much training they receive. Someone who hates working with figures may laboriously acquire the skills to do it – but he or she will never love it and won't look for opportunities to exercise that skill.

Dr. Paul Samuelson, the first American to win the Nobel Prize in economics, put it succinctly: 'Never underestimate the vital importance of finding early in life the work that for you is play. This turns possible underachievers into happy warriors.'

what do you love doing?

Although there probably are a finite number of motivated skills, only once will they come together in such a way that defines our uniqueness. Other writers use different words to describe this trait – strengths, signature strengths, dependable strengths, drivers, talents, etc. – but we'll stay with 'motivated skills' as it was the phrase Bernard Haldane used when he worked with us in the 1980s.

There is a major publishing and consulting 'industry' that has developed over the past 10 years around helping people to develop their motivated skills or strengths. The writers, researchers and consultants may not agree about what to call them but the one thing they all agree on is that people are wasting their time focusing on weaknesses and trying to fix them. How much easier and logical to focus on motivated skills and get people to become even better at doing the things they love.

But sometimes we're actively discouraged from recognising our own skills as we 'might get above ourselves'. This is not just a peculiarity of the British but certainly there have been cultural pressures not to 'show off'. And there has certainly been strong cultural pressure to spend a great deal of time and effort in improving in the areas in which we are weak.

To quote Peter Drucker again: 'It takes far more energy and work to improve from incompetence to mediocrity than it takes to improve from first rate performance to excellent.'

You will only be doing work you love by using your motivated skills so it's vital to find out what they are. People who are doing the work they love sometimes use phrases such as 'being in the zone' or 'going with the flow'. They report a level of total involvement in what they are doing that renders time irrelevant. They are at one with what they are doing. It would be wonderful to feel that in all of the work that we do, but that is unrealistic: there will always be grunt work. The trick is to ensure that this represents only a small portion of our working time.

Creativity expert Ken Robinson sums up this feeling very well:
'One of the strongest signs of being in the zone is the sense of freedom and of authenticity. When we are doing

something that we love and are naturally good at, we are much more likely to feel centred in our true sense of self – to be who we feel we truly are. When we are in 'our Element', we feel we are doing what we are meant to be doing and being who we're meant to be.'[2]

Activity 3: List Your Achievements

An achievement in this activity must satisfy three criteria:
- You did it well.
- You enjoyed it.
- You felt proud of it.

This is not easy for many of us. Generally we're not taught to think about what we've achieved and some of us still have problems in defining what we're good at, what we're proud of and what we enjoy. It is now time to shake off those shackles of humility and modesty. Each one of us has achieved much and the sum of our achievements is unique to each of us. We may not have generated world peace or a cure for AIDS, but we all will have a variety of things in our lives about which we should feel proud.

Research has demonstrated that the simple act of recalling and talking about our achievements helps us to feel more positive. This may not be very surprising, but it's interesting to note how infrequently people actually do this simple exercise when the potential benefits are so great.
- On a separate sheet of paper, write down what you think your biggest achievement is in your life so far. Also put down how old you were at the time. Now think of other achievements. Go back to when you were under 10.
- Think back to your teenage years, your time at school, further education or training. Picture yourself in your first job, then all of the other jobs you have had.
- What were you doing outside of your paid work?

2 Ken Robinson and Lou Aronica, The Element: How Finding Your Passion Changes Everything (Allen Lane, 2009).

- What did you achieve at hobbies, social activities, unpaid work and leisure pursuits?
- What were your achievements within your networks of family and friends?
- What did you learn to do?
- Did you help others?
- Did you teach others?
- Did you manage or organise or lead others?
- Did you make or create something?
- Did you travel somewhere?
- Did you persuade someone about something?
- Did you communicate really well at some point?
- Did you perform?
- Did you research something really well?
- Did you persist with a plan until you actually got what you wanted?

on a separate sheet of paper

Remember to put the age you were at the time next to each achievement.

By now you should have filled up quite a lot of that sheet of paper. If not, ask some friends, a partner, parents or other family members. Explain that you are doing this to discover what you are really good at. You could offer to do the same for them at a later date.

work and happiness

Activity 4: Rank Order Your Achievements

Look at your list and tick the seven achievements you are most proud of, you did well and you enjoyed the most. Write them below starting with what you consider to be your number 1 achievement.

1. _____
2. _____
3. _____
4. _____
5. _____
6. _____
7. _____

You can always add some additional achievements if you feel that seven is not enough.

Activity 5: What are the Most Common Motivated Skills?

Below you will see a list of 27 of the most commonly recalled motivated skills plus three blanks in case you have used skills that are not in our list. Use the blanks to write in any skills that you have used to create your achievements that are not in the list of 27.

My motivated skill is:	My motivated skill is:	My motivated skill is:
Giving credit to others Recognising and appreciating the achievements of others	**Sensitivity** Understanding the feelings of others and able to make people feel comfortable, intuitive	**Managing time** Setting priorities, making lists, working to schedules, keeping to appointments
Innovating Creating, innovating, seeing alternatives, developing new ideas	**Teaching** Teaching, training, coaching, mentoring	**Analysing** Managing and organising information, examining, dissecting, sorting through
Reviewing Able to stand back and learn from an experience	**Working creatively** With ideas, spaces, shapes, events, faces; thinking laterally	**Selling** Persuading, influencing, negotiating, promoting change
Solving problems Diagnosing, researching, assessing pros and cons	**Motivating & leading** Inspiring and energising others to achieve	**Adaptability** Flexible, expecting and welcoming change, can live with ambiguity

work and happiness

My motivated skill is:	My motivated skill is:	My motivated skill is:
Organising people Managing and organising people to get tasks done	**Strategic thinking** Able to stand back, see the big picture, construct the pictures of the future	**Performing** In a group, on stage, one to one, using showmanship
Helping others Committed to and good at doing things and providing good service to others	**Managing money** Organising finances, budgeting, keeping records	**Improvising** Adapting, experimenting, trial and error
Being practical Making things, constructing things, mending them	**Using technology** Using computers and mobile electronic devices	**Curiosity** Having an enquiring mind, keen to pursue new knowledge, questioning
Physical activities Sports, travelling, outdoor activities	**Networking** Knowing how to make contacts and to market oneself and others	**Asserting** Telling people what we want or prefer clearly and confidently without threats or putting ourselves down
High energy Is able to take on lots of projects, is rarely tired	**Persisting** Does not give up easily, hangs on in there	**Communicating** With words, written, face to face, in groups, blogging, etc.

live happier: the ultimate life skill

My motivated skill is:	My motivated skill is:	My motivated skill is:

Now look at the table on page 109. You will see along the top the references to each of your seven achievements from page 107.

You should now look down the Motivated Skills column and ask yourself: 'Did I use this skill to help me to get my number 1 achievement?'

Use your imagination. Take yourself back to the age and the time when you created that achievement. Ask yourself: 'What did I do to make that happen?'

Never ask yourself 'why?'

Do this for all of your achievements. This activity will enable you to look at the greatest achievements in your life to date so that you can discover which motivated skills you use most often. Tick each skill that you recall using that helped you to reach that achievement.

work and happiness

My Achievements

Motivated Skills	1	2	3	4	5	6	7	Totals
Giving credit to others								
Sensitivity								
Managing time								
Innovating								
Teaching								
Analysing								
Reviewing								
Working creatively								
Selling								
Solving Problems								
Motivating & leading								

Motivated Skills	1	2	3	4	5	6	7	Totals
Adaptability								
Organising people								
Strategic thinking								
Performing								
Helping others								
Managing money								
Improvising								
Being practical								
Using technology								
Curiosity								
Physical activities								
Networking								
Asserting								

Motivated Skills	1	2	3	4	5	6	7	Totals
High energy								
Persisting								
Communicating								

Count up the number of ticks that you have in each row and put the total into the end 'Totals' column.

Which are the six or seven skills that you used the most? Write them below:

1. _____
2. _____
3. _____
4. _____
5. _____
6. _____

These represent the skills that when you use them make you feel good, fulfilled and alive. These are the skills you are motivated to use. Success for you will result from using these skills. Don't waste your time trying to develop skills that don't produce this effect. So many people spend time attempting to compensate for their weaknesses when they should be getting even better at using their motivated skills.

'Knowledge of which skills are motivated gives you a handle on how to use them, develop them, train and educate them, combine them in different ways to meet changing job and educational demands.'
Bernard Haldane, Career Development Pioneer

Activity 6: How Much Opportunity Do You Have to Use Your Motivated Skills?

- Reflect now on just how many of your motivated skills you are using currently. Look again at your top six or seven motivated skills in order of importance to you and ask yourself how far that skill is used in your existing job. If you have more than one job, ask the same question for that. Next, see if you can visualise a job or jobs that you think you might enjoy.
- In the table below put the job titles in the top row and then ask yourself the question: **'How much opportunity does this job give me for using this motivated skill?'**
- If your present job allows you to fully utilise that skill, award it a 10. If it does not allow you to use it all, award it a 0. And, of course, all points in between.
- Do the same for any jobs you might be considering.
- You will see that the table gives a weighting for your scores. So, for example, if 'teaching' was your number 1 motivated skill that would appear first and you would rate that. If you had a reasonable opportunity to use that skill you might give it an 8. In the table that would be multiplied by 7 so would give you a score of 56. Do this for each of your motivated skills for each job until you have totals for each one.

My Job(s) and My Motivated Skills

My Motivated Skills	Job 1	Job 2	Job 3	Job 4	Job 5
1	_X 7 =	_X 7 =	_X 7 =	_X 7 =	_X 7 =
2	_X 6 =	_X 6 =	_X 6 =	_X 6 =	_X 6 =
3	_X 5 =	_X 5 =	_X 5 =	_X 5 =	_X 5 =
4	_X 4 =	_X 4 =	_X 4 =	_X 4 =	_X 4 =
5	_X 3 =	_X 3 =	_X 3 =	_X 3 =	_X 3 =
6	_X 2 =	_X 2 =	_X 2 =	_X 2 =	_X 2 =

My Motivated Skills	Job 1	Job 2	Job 3	Job 4	Job 5
7	_X 1 =	_X 1 =	_X 1 =	_X 1 =	_X 1 =
	Total	Total	Total	Total	Total

If you gave 10 points for each of your seven motivated skills your maximum total would be 280, although it is highly unlikely that anyone would achieve 280.

Now answer the following questions for yourself:

1. How much opportunity is there overall in your current job for you to use your motivated skills?

_____
_____
_____
_____

2. Do any of the other jobs that you have analysed more closely fit your motivated skills?

_____
_____
_____
_____

3. How do the jobs compare in the scoring?

4. Does this feel right? If not, why not? Remember intuition is just as important as numbers (probably more so).

5. Do your answers suggest questions that you might wish to ask at a job interview?

_____
_____
_____
_____

'We don't know who we can be until we know what we can do.'
Ken Robinson, Author, Speaker and Educational Adviser

The novelist George Eliot said:
'It's never too late to be what you might have been.'

'Successful careers develop when people are prepared for opportunities because they know their strengths, their method of work and their values. Knowing where one belongs can transform an ordinary person – hardworking but otherwise mediocre – into an outstanding performer.'
Peter Drucker, Social Ecologist

All of this is also true for unpaid work and voluntary activities.

Activity 7: Taking Your Motivated Skills into Unpaid Work

Think of all of the work that you do which is unpaid – at home, for the family, in voluntary groups, your hobbies, social activities, etc. Some people find it difficult to value unpaid work and yet this can sometimes involve using as many skills as those needed for paid work. If you are considering re-entering the world of paid work it is often useful to have examples of voluntary work to talk and write about which demonstrate your underlying transferable skills and their application to the benefit of the community.

If you do not currently have paid work then complete the skills exercise to identify those skills that you are using in everyday life.

If you have paid work are there are any differences between your paid work skills and your unpaid work skills?

Most of us at some point will cease paid work either by choice or necessity. When this happens it will be valuable to find other ways of using these skills. Even if you are in full-time paid work right now it is useful preparation to begin to think of what you can choose to do.

Look at your list of motivated skills

Now take them in order and write in any ideas you may have as to how you could use each of these skills in unpaid work.

Let's take 'teaching' as an example. You could use this in a social club, in voluntary work with learners (young and old), in a church study group, when travelling with a group, in a situation where you are teaching others about something of which you have specialist knowledge – sporting expertise, using the internet, playing a card game, cooking, gardening, etc.

have another look

See how many ideas you can come up with for using your motivated skills in unpaid work.

Motivated Skill	How I Use It Now	How Else I Might Use It
1.		
2.		
3.		
4.		
5.		
6.		
7.		

work and happiness

Life Skill: Know Your Life Values

There would appear to be a significant and global shift in values. Ronald Inglehart and his colleagues from the University of Michigan have been tracking and comparing public opinion across many countries for several decades. His World Values Survey, which covers 85 per cent of the world's population, has year on year noted greater concern for spiritual and non-material matters.

Daniel Pink[3] talks of 'meaning being the new money'. Victor Frankl, 50 years ago noted that 'People have enough to live, but nothing to live for; they have the means but no meaning.'

Peter Drucker, as always, has something significant to say about the importance of living by your values. He constructed what he liked to call 'the mirror test'. He recalls an incident in 1906 when the highly respected German Ambassador in London abruptly resigned rather than preside over a dinner given by the diplomatic corps for Edward VII. The King was a notorious womaniser and made it clear what kind of dinner he wanted. The Ambassador is reported to have said, 'I refuse to see a pimp in the mirror in the morning when I shave.' This mirror test asks us can we live comfortably with ourselves.

'What kind of person do I want to see in the mirror in the morning?'

Happiness and Values

Professor Ed Diener says a key component of 'living happier' is 'having goals aligned with our values'.

So, how do we find 'value-based happiness'?

---

3 Daniel H. Pink, A Whole New Mind: Why Right Brainers Will Rule the Future (Marshall Cavendish, 2008).

Our Life Values

As we grow up we absorb 'messages' and influences from our parents, our families, our teachers, our friends and eventually from society itself, from the media and the culture we engage with. We emerge as adults with our own selection of beliefs, preferences, priorities about what matters to us, what is most important for us to do, to be, to have, to aspire to, to work for. Each of us has a unique combination of values that influence and shape our decisions, and our behaviours and perhaps that will influence how satisfied and happy we will be with our life and all it involves.

Values are that important because they affect how we judge and evaluate our experiences. For example, if we value integrity we will not be happy in circumstances that involve deceit or double-dealing. If we prize challenge and adventure we are unlikely to survive in a routine or bureaucratic context.

Living a life or following a career that is aligned with our values is much more likely to result in high levels of satisfaction, motivation, commitment, health and well-being, and – probably – happiness.

Activity 8: What are Your Life Values?

Whenever we ask ourselves questions like...
- How do I like to spend my time?
- What kind of people do I choose to have around me?
- Where do I want to live and to work?

ask yourself

How important to me is money, status, independence, creativity, making decisions, taking risks, helping others, security, success, etc.... we are asking ourselves questions about our values. Being able to answer questions like these, therefore, will always be crucial to enable us to make our life more like we want it to be. The more we are able to live out our values, the more rewarding our life will be.

We may be highly competent in a particular area, but if what we are doing is not in line with our values it is unlikely to be satisfying.

Our values become apparent early on in life and are more stable than attitudes and interests. Our values are what drive us and motivate us to do or not to do certain things and to make choices every day – some small and some momentous.

This activity is an opportunity for you to clarify your key life values.

This activity will:
- Invite you to reflect on values that people have said are influential in life generally and decide how much they might apply to you.
- Ask you to identify values that may not be included but you are aware influence your decisions and your choices.
- Ask you to identify up to eight life values that are most important to you and how your life currently measures up to them.

work and happiness

Reflect on each of the following life values. As you do so, ask yourself:
- How important is this in my life as a whole? How much does it shape my decisions and my actions?
- Give each value a score from 1 to 5 based on the following:

1. = If you decide it is not one of your values and doesn't influence what you pursue or how you operate at all.
2. = If it is of little importance to you.
3. = If it is of some importance to you and shapes some of your decisions.
4. = If it is rather important to you and definitely does affect what you decide and what you do.
5. = If it most definitely is important to you and certainly does drive your decisions and actions.

Life Values. What Drives Your Life?

Ambition – you aspire to high achievement, status or standing.   Score

Integrity – you are committed to honesty and high moral standards.   Score

Relationships – you place high importance on the quality and maintenance of your relationships with friends and family.   Score

Helping society – you like to be involved in things which will make a contribution to the community, society or the world.   Score

Artistic – you appreciate art, music, design, books, theatre, film, etc.   Score

Reputation – you prize being held in high esteem for your qualities and achievements.   Score

Work-Life Balance – you want a balance between your paid work and all the other areas of your life.   Score

Spirituality – you have a sense of and a commitment to 'a greater good', to a better world, to a common humanity, to a just and healthy society, to a planet at peace.   Score

Contact with people – you enjoy having a lot of contact and interaction with people.   Score

Health and well-being – you are committed to a lifestyle which best ensures your physical and mental well-being.   Score

Stability – you value permanence and continuity in your relationships and your activities.   Score

Teamwork – you like working with others and collective achievement.   Score

work and happiness

Excitement – you need a lot of excitement
in your life.   Score

Physical challenge – you enjoy doing
something that is physically demanding. Score

Pleasure – the 'good things in life', fun and
enjoyment and time for them matter a great
deal to you.   Score

Making decisions – you like making decisions
about how things should be done, who should
do it and by when.   Score

Community – you like living in a place that
gives you ready access to activities and people
you value (e.g. social contacts, leisure, learning,
entertainment, church, etc.)   Score

Challenge – you like being stretched, adventure,
new ground, responding to the unexpected.   Score

Independence – you like being independent,
a free agent, in charge of your own life
and options.   Score

Wealth – it matters to you to have a healthy
bank balance and significant assets.　　　Score

Learning – it is important to you to
continually learn new things.　　　Score

Being expert – you like being known as someone
with special knowledge or skills.　　　Score

Helping others – you like to help other people
individually or in groups.　　　Score

Persuading people – you enjoy persuading
people to change their minds, buy something,
volunteer for something, etc.　　　Score

Security – you like to live free of fear or
anxiety with no financial worries in a safe,
unthreatening environment.　　　Score

Risk – you like to take physical, financial,
emotional or intellectual risks.　　　Score

Peace – you prefer to have few pressures or
uncomfortable demands.　　　Score

work and happiness

Communication – you enjoy being able to
express ideas well in writing or in speech.   Score

Time freedom – you prefer to be able to
choose your own times for doing things.   Score

Creative – thinking up new ideas and ways of
doing things is important to you.   Score

Competition – you like competing against other
people or groups.   Score

Variety – you like to have lots of different
things to do.   Score

live happier: **the ultimate life skill**

Now in the space below write in any life values that you know you have that are not included above and score them as above.

Life value _____	Score ___
Life value _____	Score ___
Life value _____	Score ___

Look at all the values that you have given a 5 or a 4. These are your most highly rated.

If your list contains too many equally valued items look at the list of YOUR MOST HIGHLY VALUED and reduce it to YOUR EIGHT KEY VALUES.

work and happiness

Rank them here in order of importance to you:

1. _____
2. _____
3. _____
4. _____
5. _____
6. _____
7. _____
8. _____

rank them in order

Life Skill: Match Your Work To Your Values

You will know your current job well and have some idea whether it reflects your life values. This exercise will help you to be clearer whether this is so.

It may be that your choice of job or career would normally meet most of your key values. However, where you are working and who you are working for, can be the source of dissatisfaction and the cause of problems. In which case, your choice might be to change employers rather than to change job or career.

The exercise enables you to rank up to five possible new jobs that you are interested in.

Remember, this will only tell you about the job in general and will not give you information on the actual job with that employer. For that you need to talk with people who work there or have worked there. Speak to their customers. Look at the company's website or talk directly to the employer.

Knowing your life values **can** help you to shape the questions you may want to ask when you get to an interview.

Employers generally welcome being asked about the jobs they offer because they too want to ensure that the job you apply for is the right one for you.

- Look at the list of ranked values that you have identified as VERY IMPORTANT and those that you have said are NOT IMPORTANT to you at all.
- Ask yourself how far does your present job satisfy each work value?
    1. If that value is never satisfied by your job award it 0 points.
    2. If that value is totally satisfied award it 10 points.
    3. Please use the full range from 0 to 10.
       You will see that a weighting of your answers has already been filled in for you. Simply complete the calculations. For example:
       $6 \times 8 = 48$
       $8 \times 7 = 56$
       $2 \times 6 = 12$, etc.
- Now do the same for any other jobs you might be considering.
- Add up the totals for each job you have analysed.

If you gave 10 points for each of your EIGHT VERY IMPORTANT life values your maximum total would be 360 although it is highly unlikely that anyone would achieve 360.

Very Important	My Present Job	Job / Option No. 2	Job / Option No. 3	Job / Option No. 4	Job / Option No. 5
1	_X 8 =	_X 8 =	_X 8 =	_X 8 =	_X 8 =
2	_X 7 =	_X 7 =	_X 7 =	_X 7 =	_X 7 =
3	_X 6 =	_X 6 =	_X 6 =	_X 6 =	_X 6 =
4	_X 5 =	_X 5 =	_X 5 =	_X 5 =	_X 5 =
5	_X 4 =	_X 4 =	_X 4 =	_X 4 =	_X 4 =
6	_X 3 =	_X 3 =	_X 3 =	_X 3 =	_X 3 =
7	_X 2 =	_X 2 =	_X 2 =	_X 2 =	_X 2 =
8	_X 1 =	_X 1 =	_X 1 =	_X 1 =	_X 1 =
Totals					

write your scores here

work and happiness

My Not Important Values Are: Tick any of these if they feature in your present paid work activities						
Not Important	My Present Job	Job / Option No. 2	Job / Option No. 3	Job / Option No. 4	Job / Option No. 5
1					
2					
3					
4					
5					
6					
7					

This also asks for your 'Not Important' values. These are important so that later you can assess how much doing things that you do not value might actually be part of your job.

With your list of key work values you now have a tool that you can use to analyse the suitability of any job. It can help you decide whether to choose or accept a job,

Now answer the following questions for yourself:

How much opportunity is there overall in my current job for me to express my work values?

_____
_____
_____

Do any of the values in my NOT IMPORTANT column feature in my present job?

_____
_____
_____

Do any of the other jobs that I have analysed more closely fit my key values?

_____
_____
_____

work and happiness

How do the jobs compare in the scoring?

Does this feel right? If not, why not?

Do I need additional information before making a choice?

Do my answers suggest questions that I might wish to ask at a job interview?

answers these questions

Life Skill: Finding Meaningful Work

'Here is Edward Bear, coming downstairs now, bump, bump, bump, on the back of his head, behind Christopher Robin. It is, as far as he knows, the only way of coming downstairs, but sometimes he feels that there really is another way, if only he could stop bumping for a moment and think of it. And then he feels that perhaps there isn't.'

A.A. Milne, Author of Winnie-The-Pooh

work and happiness

Do you recognise this feeling? A feeling that we are 'bumping' along, without clear goals, without feeling satisfied with the way things are going. Most of us do this from time to time. It's a sign that something is not quite right for us and this will give us the opportunity to do something about it. Treasure your feelings of dissatisfaction. They are the gateway to new options.

'Bumping along' can happen in many of life's arenas but it is perhaps especially familiar to those of us in work. We can get so caught up with the "dailyness" of work life' that we forget to ask ourselves what we are getting out of it?

When we stop 'bumping' we need to ask ourselves what do we really want to get out of life? What is the purpose behind what we are doing? What has meaning for us and what is lacking in our work life?

Positive psychologists, in their studies of healthy, successful, flourishing, happier people, have found that having 'a sense of purpose', having things we feel 'passionate' about and committing to activities that give meaning to our life are very much linked to 'living happier'.

We find 'meaning' when we use our skills, qualities and strengths in supporting or serving a cause that is 'bigger' than ourselves. We want not only to 'feel' good about what we do, but to feel that we are making a difference, that we are making things 'better', that we are part of some greater, future good.

The assassinated US Presidential candidate Bobby Kennedy interviewed towards the end of his life said that he would like his epitaph to read 'He made a contribution.' As he lived he was conscious of his legacy, as, indeed, we each should be of ours.

live happier: **the ultimate life skill**

So, 'meaning' comes from using what we are best at to serve others or to participate in a cause beyond ourselves. The other side of the 'meaning' coin has a downside. Those who see their lives as 'meaningless' are more likely to experience depression, need therapy, be involved in substance abuse, and in extreme cases even contemplate suicide.

There is a game that people sometimes play with themselves. It's called 'it will be different when…
- I've passed my exams;
- the children have started school;
- my boss will let me…;
- I have a different boss;
- I take that course;
- the children have left home;
- the right job comes along;
- I have learned to…;
- the economy has picked up;
- I retire, etc.'

If you feel like Edward Bear when you think of your work, what is your version of 'it will be different when'?

Write it here:

Activity 9: What is Your Purpose?

People need a purpose. Some like to pursue a goal that benefits not only themselves but also other people or future generations. They also like to see a connection between their daily actions and their long-term goals. As Helen Keller said, true happiness comes through 'fidelity to a worthy purpose'. Those who do not have such a compelling aim may find that, as the old saying goes, 'their soul perishes'.

There are many ways to explore our purpose. One approach is to learn from the past.

Looking back on your life, can you think of three times when you have had a strong sense of purpose? You may have been raising money for a charity, caring for someone, raising a child, learning a language, planning a garden, etc. Write in the times when you had a strong sense of purpose.

1.

2.

3.

write your thoughts here

Looking at each of these times, how did you find or create a sense of purpose? How did you then work toward achieving the goal?

1.

2.

3.

Another way of discovering what is really meaningful in your life is to explore your ideal workday.

Imagine for the next few minutes that you are not restricted by time, money, age, health, status, etc. What would your 'ideal workday' be like?

- When would your workday start?
- Where would you be working?
- What would you be doing?
- Who would you be doing it with?

work and happiness

- What skills would you be using?
- What would you be working to achieve?
- Would you be doing more than one job or piece of work during the day?
- What would you earn?
- How would other people including friends and family view that type of work? Would you be part of an organisation?
- Would you be self-employed?
- Would it be a combination of types of employment and work?
- Would all the work that you do on this day be paid for?
- Would you be learning anything new?
- Would you be managing people or being managed?
- How would your work fit alongside what else is important in your life? Describe your work/life blend.
- When would you stop working?
- Would there be any other issues about work that are important to you?

Write down your answers to the questions above and now ask yourself the following questions:

What were my thoughts, feelings and reactions to doing the exercise?

What does the exercise tell me about what is really meaningful to me?

What does it tell me I feel passionate about in my work?

What is the difference between my ideal day and my reality?

How much of this ideal working day is achievable now or in the near future?

If I can't have it all, can I have some of it?

What do I need to start doing now to make this happen?

work and happiness

Activity 10: My Obituary

This might just be one of the most difficult and emotionally demanding activities in the entire book but it really will help you to focus on what is truly meaningful in your life and how much of that links to your work.

Newspapers publish obituaries that give a description and evaluation of a person's life history, achievements, key relationships, etc.

On a separate sheet of paper, write your obituary based on your current life as if you were an objective journalist. Include the time and manner of your death. It should not be more than 600 words

on a separate sheet of paper

Now ask yourself the following questions:
- How might I have liked that obituary to read?
- What can I do to ensure that my obituary will read like I would wish it to read?
- Can I think of a fitting epitaph?
- What part does paid work and unpaid work play in this?

Review all of the activities you have worked on in this chapter.

After thinking about what is there fill in the table on the following page by writing in what you want more of, less of and what you would like to keep the same in your life right now.

Paid work	More of	Less of	Keep the same
People			
Activities			
Unpaid work			
People			
Activities			
My life in general			
People			
Activities			

Pick the three that you would like to start working on right away.
1.
2.
3.

Other Life Skills Programmes that you may want to explore in the Arena of Work are:
- **Knowing your interests**
- **Preparing for retirement**

live happier: the ultimate life skill

money

great quote about money and happiness

'Whoever said that money can't buy happiness isn't spending it right.'
Advertisement for Lexus cars.

Money and Happiness

What is Known About Money and Happiness?

On the whole, richer people are happier than poorer people – but only up to certain limits. Professor Daniel Kahneman's[1] research suggests that there is a relationship between wealth and happiness. He concluded that the salary most likely to contribute to a person's happiness in the USA is $75,000 (£45,000), beyond which emotional happiness does not increase with increasing income. He suggests that the richer people become the less likely they are to enjoy the small pleasures in life to the same extent – 'a good meal or even a piece of chocolate'. He also says that the poor think the rich must be happy and the rich think that the poor must be unhappy. Neither of which is correct.

His research shows that 45 percent of the richest Americans are very happy but so are 33 per cent of the poorest. And those statistics have held true for the past 30 years. During that time the richest have doubled their standards of living. Richard Layard[2] describes this as a paradox:

'When people become richer compared with other people they become happier. But when whole societies have become richer they have not become happier.'

---

1 D. Kahneman, A. Krueger, D. Schkade, N. Schwarz, A. Stone, 'Would you be happier if you were richer? A focusing illusion.' Science, 312, 5782 (2006), 1908-1910.
2 Richard Layard, Happiness – Lessons from a New Science (Penguin, 2005).

Comparison appears to be a crucial variable in whether people are happy with what they have. In families, it has been found that the more your partner earns than you, the less satisfied you will be with your own job.[3] Among women, if your sister's husband is earning more than your husband then you are more likely to look to earn more.

Comparisons in this case, as in so many walks of life, are odious. Don't compare yourself with people who are more successful than you are. Always compare downwards not upwards. Some fascinating research[4] shows that the more TV you watch the more you are likely to overestimate the affluence of others. We see too many people buying or owning too many things.

Interestingly, most people find it more satisfying to give than receive. Those who spent more of their income on others rather than themselves were much happier.[5] There is some evidence to suggest that people with lower self-esteem tend to be far more materialistic and, therefore, less happy.[6]

One of the extraordinary findings from many research studies states that we hate losing things more than gaining things. This is why people cannot bring themselves to sell shares that have plummeted, or houses whose value has depreciated. We just hold on waiting for things to improve – and of course get more and more unhappy as our position deteriorates.

Daniel Kahneman asked people if they would risk £100 for the chance to win a larger sum. What potential sum would make you risk that £100?

---

3   A.E. Clark, 'L'utilite est-elle relative? Analyse a l'aide de donnees sur les ménages', Economie et Provision, (1996), 121, 151–64.
4   J. Schou, The Overspent American: Upscaling, Downshifting and the New Consumer (Harper Collins, 1999).
5   E.W. Dunn, L. Aknin and M.I. Norton, 'Spending money on others promotes happiness', Science, 319 (2008), 1687–88.
6   L.N. Chaplin and D.R. John, 'Growing up in a material world: age differences in materialism in children and adolescents', Journal of Consumer Research, 34(4) (2007), 480–94.

money and happiness

The typical answer is around £200. People need the prospect of gaining twice £100 to outweigh the chance of losing £100. And if you think that's odd watch the TED talk by Laurie Santos who describes her experiments with monkeys which demonstrates that we are not really much superior to them when it comes to monkeynomics: www.ted.com/talks/view/lang/eng//id/927.

One other important research finding is that as far as happiness is concerned you will do better buying someone an experience rather than a 'thing'. And this also applies to what you spend your money on for yourself.[7] We also know that people who spend more money on others than on themselves are happier.[8]

So – Can We Buy Happiness?

To some degree we can but it depends how we spend it. If we have more money then we can get more control over our lives – in theory. But many people simply carry on amassing more and not using it for others or even for themselves. We have already discussed that spending on others will get us more happiness than spending on ourselves. We know that comparing ourselves with others even better off will certainly not make us live happier. We also apparently tend to spend the most when we feel the worst.

Many of us only have a rough estimate of what we spend and the first activity will provide a simple spreadsheet to enable you to get an accurate picture of your current financial situation.

get a picture of your finances

---

7 L. Van Boven and T. Gilovich, 'To do or to have: That is the question', Journal of Personality and Social Psychology, 85(6) (2003), 1193–1202.
8 E.W. Dunn, L. Aknin and M.I. Norton, 'Spending money on others promotes happiness', Science, 319 (2008), 1687–88.

Knowing what income we have and what we spend is only the first step. Another activity asks you to begin to assess just what returns you are getting from the ways you spend your money and your time. If you want more out of life than you are currently getting then one of your options may be to cut down on the time you are doing paid work. This probably means, however, that you will have to cut down on your expenditure. This activity should enable you to make decisions as to how to simplify your life and live with less income if you so choose.

Activity 1: What Do I Earn, What Do I Spend and What Do I Need?

A major barrier to us getting what we want out of life is the belief that: **'I cannot afford to live on less than I earn or get now.'**

This activity will help you to record specific data on your outgoings and your income and then, crucially, invites you to assess just what you get from each of these expenditures.

We have included a spreadsheet for you to use. You can use the one below but you may be better off creating your own so that you can write in your own categories. If you have a computer with a spreadsheet this would be the ideal way of doing it. Any spreadsheet will work. We did one for the learndirect site:
http://community.learndirect.co.uk/community/docs/DOC-1156.

Martin Lewis also has a good one here:
www.moneysavingexpert.com/banking/Budget-planning.

money and happiness

WARNING: The next piece of work does involve considerable preparation to be able to complete it accurately and it can be ongoing.

We suggest that you budget for a year. Look at your bills for last year, your direct debits, your cheque books and bank statements. Look at gas, electricity, water charges. Look at your council tax charges, your rent/mortgage outgoings, etc. Work out the totals for the year and place a 12th in each month. Estimate for the other items – money spent on: holidays, eating out, entertainment, travel, insurance, costs of running your car(s), etc. and insert the average monthly spend. Most of us underestimate what we spend on food and drink, and also on clothes and going out. See what you find.

live happier: the ultimate life skill

What You Spend

Year	Jan	Feb	Mar	Apr	May	Jun	Jul	Aug	Sep	Aug
Household										
Rent/mortgage										
Food & entertaining										
Take away meals										
Alcohol/tobacco, etc.										
House insurance										
Contents insurance										
Water rates										
House repairs										
New house items										
Telephones										
Gas										
Electricity										
Council tax										
DIY materials										
Pets										
Total										

money and happiness

Year	Sep	Oct	Nov	Dec	Total	Essential	Nice to have	Could spend less
Household								
Rent/mortgage								
Food & entertaining								
Take away meals								
Alcohol/tobacco, etc.								
House insurance								
Contents insurance								
Water rates								
House repairs								
New house items								
Telephones								
Gas								
Electricity								
Council tax								
DIY materials								
Pets								
Total								

live happier: the ultimate life skill

Year	Jan	Feb	Mar	Apr	May	Jun	Jul	Aug	Sep	Aug
Entertainment										
Books/mags/subs										
Downloads/DVDs/apps										
TV and broadband										
Gardening items										
Meals out										
Theatre/cinema/events										
Holidays										
Sports										
Learning										
Travel insurance										
Total										

money and happiness

Year	Sep	Oct	Nov	Dec	Total	Essential	Nice to have	Could spend less
Entertainment								
Books/ mags/subs								
Downloads/DVDs/apps								
TV and broadband								
Gardening items								
Meals out								
Theatre/cinema/events								
Holidays								
Sports								
Learning								
Travel insurance								
Total								

live happier: the ultimate life skill

Year	Jan	Feb	Mar	Apr	May	Jun	Jul	Aug	Sep	Aug
Family										
Child 1										
Child 2										
Child 3										
Parents										
Other family										
Friends										
Presents										
Pets										
Total										

Car/travel	Jan	Feb	Mar	Apr	May	Jun	Jul	Aug	Sep	Aug
Car tax										
Fuel										
Vehicle insurance										
Breakdown insurance										
Repayments										
Repairs/MOT										
Public transport										
Taxis										
Total										

money and happiness

Year	Sep	Oct	Nov	Dec	Total	Essential	Nice to have	Could spend less
Family								
Child 1								
Child 2								
Child 3								
Parents								
Other family								
Friends								
Presents								
Pets								
Total								

	Sep	Oct	Nov	Dec	Total	Essential	Nice to have	Could spend less
Car/travel								
Car tax								
Fuel								
Vehicle insurance								
Breakdown insurance								
Repayments								
Repairs/MOT								
Public transport								
Taxis								
Total								

Year	Jan	Feb	Mar	Apr	May	Jun	Jul	Aug	Sep	Aug
Health & hygeine										
Prescriptions										
Health/sports club,etc										
Health insurance										
Dentist, optician, etc.										
Total										

Money matters	Jan	Feb	Mar	Apr	May	Jun	Jul	Aug	Sep	Aug
Pensions										
Lottery/gambling										
Charity										
Stationery/postage										
Savings										
Insurance										
Total										

money and happiness

Year	Jan	Feb	Mar	Apr	May	Jun	Jul	Aug	Sep	Aug
Health & hygeine										
Prescriptions										
Health/sports										
club,etc										
Health insurance										
Dentist,optician, etc										
Total										

	Jan	Feb	Mar	Apr	May	Jun	Jul	Aug	Sep	Aug
Money matters										
Pensions										
Lottery/gambling										
Charity										
Stationery/postage										
Savings										
Insurance										
Total										

live happier: the ultimate life skill

Year	Jan	Feb	Mar	Apr	May	Jun	Jul	Aug	Sep	Aug
Clothes										
Clothes										
Shoes										
Dry cleaning/ laundry										
Total										

Miscellaneous			
Total			

Year	Jan	Feb	Mar	Apr	May	Jun	Jul	Aug	Sep	Aug
What you spend										
Grand total										

money and happiness

Year	Sep	Oct	Nov	Dec	Total	Essential	Nice to have	Could spend less
Clothes								
Clothes								
Shoes								
Dry cleaning/laundry								
Total								

Miscellaneous					
Total					

Year	Sep	Oct	Nov	Dec	Total	Essential	Nice to have	Could spend less
What you spend								
Grand total								

live happier: the ultimate life skill

What You Earn

Year	Jan	Feb	Mar	Apr	May	Jun	Jul	Aug	Sep	Oct	Nov	Dec	Total
Paid work													
State Benefits													
Bank Interest													
Dividends													
Premium bonds/lotteries etc													
Expenses													
Building society interest													
Gifts													
Grants or loan, other sources													
State pension													
Occupational pension													
Total													

Spending total			
Earnings total			
Balance			

livehappier.com

money and happiness

What does the picture tell you about your financial situation?

What would you like to change?

What might you need to change?

What will it take to make the changes you want or need?

Activity 2: What Am I Getting Out of Life For My Money?

It's now time to see just what you are getting for the money you are spending. At the far right of your spreadsheet is a column in which you are asked to enter one of E, N or C. These mean:

- Essential
- Nice to have
- Could spend Less

If you are using the learndirect website (http://community.learndirect.co.uk/community/docs/DOC-1156) then click on FINANCIAL HEALTH CHECK again and you will see that at the right-hand side of the table are the three columns. The headings are already there for you. Look at each item on the spreadsheet and write/type in an X by each one you believe to be essential to the way you want to live your life.

The next column asks you which of these items are 'nice to have'. Again, write/type in an X as appropriate.

The third column is asking you if you wish to spend less on that item. You can choose between giving the item:
1. = absolutely not;
2. = to some extent;
3. = significantly; or
4. = totally reduce or even eliminate that item.

Reflections

What do you realise as a result of this activity?

_____
_____
_____
_____

Are you surprised by anything that you have found from this activity?

_____
_____
_____
_____

money and happiness

What does the picture tell you about your financial situation?

What would you like to change?

live happier: the ultimate life skill

What might you need to change?

What will it take to make the changes you want or need?

money and happiness

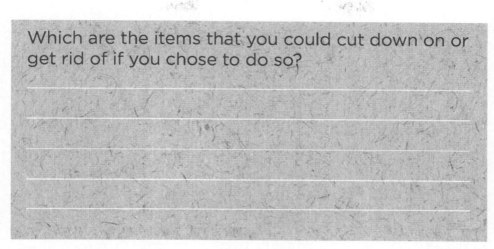

Which are the items that you could cut down on or get rid of if you chose to do so?

The challenge for you will then be to convert some of these thoughts into objectives and to develop action plans to achieve them.

Many of us trap ourselves into a lifestyle because of assumptions we make of what we must have before life is worthwhile. Our 'hunger' can sometimes be so consuming that we pursue goals which are not in our best interests and not even in line with our life values.

Activity 3: How Do I Cut Down On My Spending?

The previous activity should have helped you to identify some ways that you might cut down on your spending if you wish to do so. We are certainly not advocating that everyone should cut down on their spending. It only becomes important if the way you are currently investing your time and energies is not giving you what you want.

Tips to Save Money

- Explore what you want to buy in stores and then buy items on the internet.
- Use voucher saving schemes, loyalty cards.
- Negotiate in small business-owned stores. You can try in the larger stores but the salespeople often have no delegated power to negotiate with you.
- Ask for discounts for cash.
- Try home exchange schemes instead of renting villas and houses. Take off-peak holidays.
- Forget designer labels and go to TK Maxx, Primark, George at ASDA, etc.
- Buy second-hand. Pay off credit cards. The interest rates are horrendous.
- Use public transport instead of a car.
- Try using a carpool to get to work. Set one up. Try lift sharing: www.liftshare.com.
- Shop around for insurance cover, utilities, telephone service providers. Use www.uswitch.com or www.energyhelpline.com.
- Sign up for Martin Lewis' Money Tips email at www.moneysavingexpert.com. He also has a couple of excellent books on saving money. Buy them second-hand on Amazon.
- Don't change your car every two to three years. Keep it on the road for 10 years and run it into the ground.
- Swap services with people you know, e.g. hairdressing for babysitting, cleaning for bookkeeping, etc.
- Sign up to www.petrolprices.com for the latest pump prices at all the service stations close to your postcode.
- Use email instead of letters.
- Check that your pension or benefits are what they should be. For help with pension queries try www.pensioncalculator.org.uk. For benefits start with
http://www.turn2us.org.uk/benefits_search.aspx

money and happiness

- Lynda Gratton in her book 'The Shift' makes a crucial point about our need to earn money:

'I work ... to earn money ... which I use ... to consume stuff ... which makes me happy.'

She suggests that instead we should replace this with the following:
'I work ... to gain productive experiences ... that are the basis ... of my happiness.'

In this chapter you will have worked out:
- how much you earn and how much you spend;
- what you are getting out of your life from the money you spend.

Fill in the following table by writing in what you want more of, less of and what you would like to keep the same in your life right now.

	More of	Less of	Keep the same
Things			
Income			

Pick the three that you would like to start working on right away.
1.
2.
3.

you can start right now

live happier: the ultimate life skill

health

wise words indeed

'The greatest discovery of my generation is that human beings can alter their lives by altering their attitudes of mind.'
William James- Psychologist

 livehappier.com

Health and Happiness

What is Known About Health and Happiness?

(Please note – the information offered in this chapter is not a substitute for professional medical advice. Always regard your doctor as the source of best advice on any topics raised here.)

Is there a link between health and happiness? Does a happier life make us healthier or a healthier life make us happier? Since it is ancient wisdom that a 'healthy mind' is related to a 'healthy body' and all opinion polls show that we regard 'good health' as highly desirable, the answers would seem obvious, but the research evidence and the learning in it are intriguing.

As we ponder the following, let us recall that the message everywhere within this book and on the live happier website (www.livehappier.com) is that our happiness level is less to do with our circumstances in life and much more to do with our **attitude** to our circumstances in life. It is not to do so much with what life brings us as to what we make of what life brings us. Poor people, therefore, can be happy and wealthy people can be unhappy. Unwell people can be happy and healthy people can be unhappy and, of course, vice versa.

Positive Psychology researchers[1] explored three aspects of health and their links with happiness:
- morbidity (the incidence and frequency of ill health in individuals);
- survival (the speed and level of recovery after illness);
- longevity (the length of life).

The evidence is that:
- living happier can mean living healthier and living healthier can mean living happier;
- having a happier disposition, being optimistic, living with hope and being positive are key components of health and longevity;[2]
- happier people become ill less often, recover quicker, have fewer visits to the doctor, spend less time in hospital, and have more life and energy;
- happier people (with higher levels of positive feelings in their lives) have fewer health problems, lower death rates from cardiovascular disease, suicide, accidents, homicide, mental disorder, drug dependency, alcoholism and liver disease;
- happiness strengthens our immune systems, making us more resistant to infections, and protects against heart disease;
- depression increases the likelihood of ill health. Depressed people are several times more likely to experience heart attacks and hypertension that can lead to strokes;
- stress hastens the body's ageing process;
- a loving relationship can reduce the likelihood of men suffering from angina;

here's the evidence

---

1 See research on health and happiness reported in: Ed Diener and Robert Biswas-Diener, Happiness: Unlocking the Mysteries of Psychological Wealth (Blackwell, 2008); Martin E.P. Seligman, Authentic Happiness (Nicholas Brealey Publishing, 2003); Alan Carr, Positive psychology; the science of happiness and human strengths (Routledge, 2004).

2 D.D. Danner, D.A. Snowden and W.V. Friesen, 'Positive emotions in early life and longevity: findings from the nun study', Journal of Personality and Social Psychology, 80(5) (2001), 804–13.

health and happiness

- individuals without a good, supportive, social network are more likely to smoke, be obese and have high blood pressure. Individuals with strong social ties are more likely to be happier and survive longer following a heart attack;
- happier people (those who show higher levels of positive emotion such as love, interest, hope, gratitude, eagerness, energy, contentment, fun) live longer than those who don't demonstrate such positives;
- people who have frequent experience of joy and love in their lives live longer than those who don't, even if they have medical conditions and are smokers.

Be Optimistic, but be Careful

The survival rate of 'happier' people with the onset of a serious disease may be reduced by their positive attitude if:

- their optimism causes them to ignore early symptoms of disease and not seek speedy diagnosis and treatment (note, there is an optimal level of optimism that if exceeded can cause us to become unrealistic);
- their 'happy' state means they reject invasive, aggressive therapy, deciding quality of life is more important than length of life.

A recent sad example of this was the case of the design genius Steve Jobs whose death was much mourned. A very close colleague of Steve's wondered publicly whether Steve's self-belief and huge resolve did actually work against him in causing him to avoid seeking early medical help for his pancreatic cancer.[3]

Living happier is a great way to live and should be an ally of the best of the medical world, not a substitute for it. At the same time, it is worth noting that severely ill cancer patients can enjoy a 'life satisfaction' level that differs only slightly from that of a healthy person.

be optimistic but careful

---

3 <http://www.bbc.co.uk/news/technology-16157142>.

live happier: the ultimate life skill

The Dieners' excellent book offers us a 'quickie' checklist (adapted here) to help us ponder our approach to healthier and happier living.

Activity 1: Your Health and Happiness

Tick those that are true for you.

1. I am a non-smoker.
2. I am teetotal or drink alcohol only moderately.
3. I am a normal weight.
4. I am a careful, safe driver.
5. I use a sunscreen when needed.
6. I have a healthy diet with plenty of fruit and vegetables.
7. I monitor my health and take medication as advised.
8. I exercise regularly.
9. I practise dental hygiene.
10. I am safety conscious.
11. I am generally a happy person.

health and happiness

12. I have times of joy in my life.
13. I find my life generally satisfying.
14. I feel 'down' occasionally but soon get over it.
15. I very rarely get angry.
16. I rarely feel stressed.
17. I am grateful and trusting.
18. I have strong friendships and family ties.
19. I am sensibly optimistic.
20. I have a happy social life.

tick the boxes that are true

The suggestion is that a high score of ticks in the first 10 will indicate you are alert to and follow sound health practices. This gives you the best chance of a long and healthy life. A high score of ticks in the second 10 will probably ensure that you will 'live happier' on the journey.

Happiness and the National Health Service (NHS)

In the NHS there is a recognition that ill health is not just about smoking and drinking too much, and treatment is not all about prescribing drugs. Some health service providers[4] are recognising that living happier might be just as valuable in health and longevity terms than giving up smoking.

Dr Derek Cox says: 'We've spent years saying that giving up smoking could be the single most important thing that we could do for the health of the nation. And yet there is mounting evidence that happiness might be at least as powerful a predictor, if not a more powerful predictor, than some of the other lifestyle factors that we talk about in terms of smoking, diet, physical activity and those kind of things.... If you are happy, you are likely in the future to have less in the way of physical illness than those who are unhappy.'

Dr Cox went on to point out that people are happier if they are given more control at work, if they live in a safe neighbourhood and if they participate in community projects. Dr. Cox was part of the NHS movement to replace drug treatment for anxiety and depression by courses of cognitive behavioural therapy (CBT).

The British Heart Foundation's Professor of Psychology Andrew Steptoe claims that happier people have greater protection against heart disease and strokes. Research in the USA[5] found that happier and more optimistic people have an additional nine years of life expectancy when compared with those who are less happy.

---

4 Dr Derek Cox, Director of Public Health, Dumfries and Galloway NHS, as reported in <http://news.bbc.co.uk/1/hi/programmes/happiness_formula/4924180.stm>.
5 D.D. Danner, D.A. Snowden and W.V. Friesen, 'Positive emotions in early life and longevity: findings from the nun study', Journal of Personality and Social Psychology, 80(5) (2001), 804–13.

health and happiness

Tal Ben-Shahar taught the most popular course, Positive Psychology, at Harvard University.[6] Based on research and scientific evidence, he advises these ways to achieve a happier life:
- focus on the positive;
- make being optimistic and grateful a way of life;
- make gratitude a daily activity;
- 'exercise regularly': regular, appropriate exercise has been shown to be as effective as taking anti-depressants. Exercise is natural and necessary and increases our self-esteem and our mental functioning. It boosts our immune system, helps us to sleep better and can improve our sex life;
- 'simplify your life': time pressure, multitasking, being constantly available via new technology and over-committing is like playing several pieces of your favourite music all at the same time; result: cacophony and hassle;
- 'give yourself permission to be human': accept your emotions as part of life; all lives have downs as well as ups.

Gratitude, Optimism and Health

Grateful people tend to be more optimistic, a characteristic that researchers say boosts the immune system.
- 'There are some very interesting studies linking optimism to better immune function', says Lisa Aspinwall[7], a psychology professor at the University of Utah. In one study, researchers comparing the immune systems of healthy, first-year law students, under stress, found that by mid-term, students characterised as optimistic maintained higher numbers of blood cells that protect the immune system compared with their more pessimistic classmates.

boosts the immune system

---

6 Tal Ben-Shahar, "Cheer Up. Here's how ...," The Guardian, December 2007.
7 Aspinwall, L. G., & Tedeschi, R.G. (2010). The value of Positive Psychology for Health Psychology: Progress and pitfalls in examining the relation of positive phenomena to health. Annals of Behavioral Medicine, 39, 4-15.

- Optimism[8] also has a positive health impact on people with challenging conditions. In separate studies, patients with AIDS, as well as those preparing to undergo surgery, had better health outcomes when they maintained attitudes of optimism.
- Grateful people take better care of themselves and engage in more protective health behaviours such as regular exercise, a healthy diet, regular physical examinations.
- The work of Professors Robert Emmons and Michael McCullough shows that those who focus on the positive things in life and are grateful, feel better about life, are more optimistic, more successful in achieving what they aim for, are more helpful to other people, and have fewer physical symptoms. (http://psychology.ucdavis.edu/labs/emmons/)

Work, Health and Happiness

- A University of California study showed that people's immune systems weakened with the stress of unemployment. The immune system of those finding work showed a substantial recovery.[9]
- 'Good work' has a beneficial effect on health. 'Good work' is that which offers 'safety, fairness, job security, personal fulfilment and job satisfaction, good communications, personal autonomy and a supportive environment.'[10]
- Not all jobs are 'healthful' of course. Dr Hewett of the Centre for Work-Life Policy,[11] researches what she calls 'Extreme Jobs', those that are fast-paced and involve long hours (more than 60 hours a week). These jobs can produce the kinds and levels of stress that cause 'burnout'. The 'stressors' she identifies are:
  - rigidity in your work, together with unpredictability;
  - a fast pace and tight deadlines;
  - being 24/7 available to clients;
  - constant travel;

---

8 <http://www.mahealthcare.com/Health_Wellness/gratitude.cfm>.
9 <http://www.psychosomaticmedicine.org/content/69/3/225.full>.
10 <http://www.dwp.gov.uk/docs/hwwb-is-work-good-for-you.pdf>.
11 Sylvia Ann Hewlett and Carolyn Buck Luce, Extreme Jobs: The Dangerous Allure of the 70-Hour Workweek <http://www.worklifepolicy.org/index.php/section/research_pubs>.

health and happiness

- work-related events outside working hours;
- frustrating interruptions during the working day due to intrusive modern communications.
- Health and work are linked. The long-term unemployed are three times more likely to suffer long-term illness or disability than those in managerial and professional occupations. Those who have never worked are six times more likely.[12]

So, if our health can contribute to our happiness and our happiness can contribute to our health, then we need to give attention to them both. To live healthier we need to attend to:

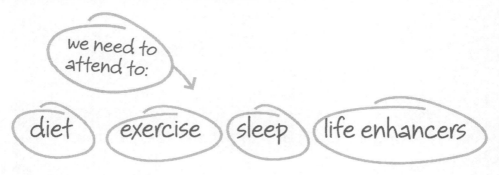

Activity 2: Healthy Living and Diet - What Do I Know?

Today there is a huge amount of coverage in the media of the latest health research and findings. We are bombarded by advice on what it takes to get healthy and stay healthy.
But how much do we KNOW of the details behind the advice and how much do we DO about it?

---

12 <http://www.dwp.gov.uk/docs/health-and-work-handbook.pdf>.

Consider each of the statements below and mark it with a T if you believe it to be TRUE or with an F if you decide it to be FALSE. The answers and sources of information on the internet are listed below.

Diet

1. Men can safely drink up to three pints of beer, or four shorts, or two large glasses of wine aday and women can drink up to two pints, or two large glasses of wine, or four shorts or cocktails a day.

2. The UK recommended daily calorie intake is 2,550 for men and 1,940 for women.

3. As long as we keep below the recommended daily calorie intake it doesn't really matter much what we eat.

4. Being overweight or obese is very likely to be damaging to health and well-being.

5. Being overweight is all due to our genetic makeup.

6. We should all know our Body Mass Index (BMI) to recognise whether we are overweight.

7. To stay healthy we should all eat at least 5 portions of fruit and vegetables every day (not including potatoes).

health and happiness

8. Saturated fats (found in dairy products, red meat, palm and coconut oils) and hydrogenated fats (found in fast food, types of margarines, commercial cakes and biscuits) should be avoided, though monounsaturated and polyunsaturated fats (found in olive oil, some nut oils and oily fish) can be beneficial.

9. Some carbohydrates (potatoes especially fried, pizza, refined cereals, sugar, soft drinks, white bread, white rice) are to be eaten sparingly, while others (brown rice, whole grains, whole fruits, legumes, whole wheat products) are much more beneficial.

10. Protein is best obtained from fish, trimmed poultry, lean meat, eggs, beans, nuts, grains and a variety of vegetables.

11. Taking vitamins and other food supplements is essential.

How did you do? Check your answers.

live happier: the ultimate life skill

1.  The above levels of intake are likely to take the drinkers above the safety limits recommended by the NHS. See: www.nhs.uk/livewell/alcohol/Pages/Alcoholhome.aspx.

Some other countries have higher recommended alcohol levels.

2.

3.  A balanced healthy diet requires more vegetables and less salt, sugar and saturated fats than a typical diet. See: www.nhs.uk/livewell/Pages/Livewellhub.aspx.

4.  Obesity significantly reduces life expectancy and is linked to a range of health problems. Report: www.nhs.uk/conditions/obesity/Pages/introduction.aspx.

5.  While there are links being established between certain genes and the likelihood of a person becoming obese, the most common cause of increasing obesity is still regarded as inappropriate diet and lack of exercise. www.nhs.uk/conditions/obesity/Pages/Introduction.aspx).

6.  It should be part of our health awareness. You can use the BMI Calculator to check whether you are the advised weight for your height. www.eufic.org/article/en/rid/eufic-bmi-calculator

health and happiness

7.  true   Take the five-a-day quiz on www.nhs.uk/Livewell/5ADAY/Pages/Why5ADAY.aspx.

8.  true

9.  true

10.  true

11.  false   We may only need these if our diet is deficient in any way or if we have a medical condition and they are prescribed. www.nhsdirect.nhs.uk/en/Search?q=vitamins&filter=Allwww.nhsdirect.nhs.uk.

Remember, living happier probably means avoiding being over obsessive about diet. Eat sensibly, enjoy the process and the conviviality that can be part of it.[13]

---

13 Any data not accredited is based on the excellent 'Living Better, Living Longer – the Secrets of Healthy Ageing'. A special health report by the Harvard Medical School.

live happier: the ultimate life skill

Activity 3: Eating to Live Happier

How would you describe the quality of your present diet? Tick the box that best describes your diet.

Enjoyable and Healthy ☐

Enjoyable but not very Healthy ☐

Enjoyable but not at all Healthy ☐

If you are have not ticked the top box write in three things you could do to make your diet more Enjoyable and Healthy.

_____
_____
_____

Which will you do? When will you start?

livehappier.com

Activity 4: Use It or Lose It

'If there is anything close to a fountain of youth it is exercise. Given its proven benefits and low side-effect profile, if it were a pill everybody would be on it!'
Dr Anne Fabiny, Assistant Professor of Medicine, Harvard Medical School

Again, consider each of the statements below and enter T for TRUE or F for FALSE after each statement to see how well you do.

The following can result from building appropriate exercise into our daily life:

Stronger heart and lungs.

Increased respect from other people.

Increase of 'good' and decrease of 'bad' cholesterol in our blood stream.

Increase in energy levels and feeling of refreshment resulting from increased intake of oxygen.

Appearing sexier.

Reduction in high blood pressure.

Improved sight and hearing.

Strengthening of muscles and bones.

Improvement in balance and coordination.

Delayed baldness.

Maintenance of healthy body weight.

Desire to eat more desserts.

Prevention and management of diabetes.

Improved mood.

Increased libido.

Improved coping with pain, stress and depression.

Injury or worse.

Improvement in how we look and feel.

Reduced risk of certain cancers.

Better sleep.

Longer life.

health and happiness

How did you do?

In fact research suggests that all the benefits of regular exercise listed are **True** except for:
- improved sight and hearing;
- appearing sexier;
- delayed baldness;
- increased respect from other people...

...which as yet seem to be unproven. Still, it seems that exercise is full of promise!

How Much Exercise?

Research,[14] then, has shown that all the benefits identified as True can result from introducing a moderate amount of exercise into our daily life except hopefully 'Injury or worse'. See: www.health.harvard.edu/special_health_reports/exercise.

That is included in the True column to ensure that we do not unwisely move too quickly from a life of low physical activity to one of energetic exercise. Please note the following:

- Healthy exercise does NOT mean training like an Olympic athlete or professional sportsperson or becoming obsessive about an exercise regime.
- Embarking on a new exercise programme, if we don't have a history of exercise, should be done with caution.
- If we are not used to exercise advice should be taken from our doctor and if given the go-ahead we should proceed with caution and build up slowly.

---

14 <http://www.health.harvard.edu/special_health_reports/exercise>.

- Unused muscles tear easily, joints are likely to be less flexible, ligaments less tolerant. Take advice on your medical readiness and do not overdo it.

The need is not for overexertion or the level of exercise that makes us tired, sweaty, out of breath or in pain. Our aim should rather be for 'active living'. For example:

- Moderate activity with which we are comfortable (the kind that makes us warm and makes us breathe a bit more deeply – the equivalent of brisk walking).
- Activity which invigorates rather than tires us (can include gardening, mowing the lawn, playing with children or grandchildren, climbing the stairs, housework, gentle dancing, swimming or cycling).
- 30 minutes a day, or most days (not necessarily all in one go: 3 x 10 minutes in the day can ease us in to it).

See: www.nhs.uk/Livewell/fitness/Pages/Fitnesshome.aspx

health and happiness

Here are some more tips if you decide to take up exercise.

Warm up gradually before any exercise to prepare the body for increased activity. Gentle stretching exercises for the different areas of the body will protect against strains and pulled muscles. And most importantly do warm down exercises after the activities.
Aerobic exercise, which raises our heart and lung rate, is very important and valuable. If you are new to it **take medical advice first**, and if given the go-ahead try brisk walking, biking or swimming.
Start with moderate exercise (say 30 minutes of brisk walking) four to five days a week.
Brisk walking means walking as if you are late for an appointment and you are slightly out of breath. You should be able to walk and talk at the same time; if you can't talk you are probably overdoing it!
The best fitness regimes include aerobic exercises, flexibility exercises and strengthening exercises.
A regularly active life, gardening, walking, energetic housework, dancing, using stairs not lifts, carrying shopping, etc. can be as valuable as an exercise programme.
Exercise with others, preferably with good-fun friends – the social element will help the motivation and the enjoyment.
Listening to music while exercising can be a very pleasant accompaniment.
Vary your activity programme. Changing activities, varying venues and routes, trying something new, can revive energy and interest.
Decide what is the best time of day for your body. Some of us are best in the morning, some in the evening and all points in between.
Eating healthily and always keeping your body hydrated will be the essential basis for regular physical activity.
Wear appropriate clothes for the exercise you are doing as they can really help. They will increase your comfort and can reduce injury, especially footwear suited to your activity.
Check your pulse frequently during exercise to make sure you are not overdoing it. http://www.bhf.org.uk/heart-health/tests/checking-your-pulse.aspx

Stop exercising immediately if you experience severe shortage of breath, coughing, pain or chest discomfort, dizziness, nausea or any other unusual symptoms and consult your doctor.
Don't exercise in extremes of temperature, with a full stomach or when you are unwell.
Choose activities you enjoy because if you don't your enthusiasm will soon wane.
Cool down slowly; between five and 10 minutes of gentle movement and stretching exercises to round off the greater exertions will help the body to ease itself back to normal.

tick which applies to you

How would you describe your present level of physical fitness?

Not great   Reasonable   One I am happy with

If you have said you are not happy with your fitness level and would like to be so, what could you do to safely increase it?

_____

_____

And when? _____

health and happiness

Sleep
Activity 5: Sleep Well

An important element in our well-being, often ignored, is a good night's sleep. It seems that seven hours sleep is the optimum number of hours. A six-year study showed that those who slept seven hours per night had the lowest rate of mortality, those who slept for more than seven had the highest. Enough, it seems, is healthier than too much.[15] Over-sleeping can be a symptom of depression as can insomnia.

We have only to experience the results of a lack of sleep to know for certain that it is not a happy condition. Not sleeping well over an extended period most certainly damages our well-being. We probably lie awake worrying and rise exhausted. We look and feel weary and worn out, our brain feels scrambled, we are often grumpy and impatient, we can't concentrate, the structure of our life suffers and so does our work or our learning and perhaps also our relationships. We are all likely to have some sleepless nights, but it is the persistent problem that can impact greatly on us.

The causes of our sleeplessness may be many: stress at work or at home, or both; money worries; illness; losing our job; losing our partner; becoming a parent; worrying over our children; a challenge or crisis looming and so on. We may lose sleep through over-stimulation: clubbing, having to prepare a presentation, computer gaming into the night, over indulgence. Whatever the cause, the result is likely to be damaging.

lack of sleep is never good

15 Report in The Observer Health Magazine, July 2008.

live happier: the ultimate life skill

'Making $60,000 more in annual income has less of an effect on your daily happiness than getting one extra hour of sleep a night.'

Professor Norbert Schwarz, Psychologist

health and happiness

Losing sleep over time can:
- affect our health;
- increase our risk of anxiety and depression;
- reduce our body's ability to heal itself;
- hasten premature ageing;
- increase our stress level;
- increase the risk of accidents;
- reduce our quality of life; and
- reduce our happiness.

'Living with poor sleep ... is in all likelihood degrading Britain's health. This is not a trivial matter. It's time for the NHS to pay attention to the scientific evidence that persistent poor sleep elevates the risk of developing new illnesses ... such as diabetes, but also very convincingly depression.'
Professor Colin Espie, Glasgow University and Co-founder of Sleepio

What to Do

In severe cases of insomnia, of course, we do need to see our doctor.

Short of that, what can we do to help ourselves? The Mayo Clinic[16] offers these tips (adapted):

1. **Have a sleep routine** – go to bed and get up at about the same times to help your body develop a consistent sleep-wake cycle. If you are not asleep in 15 minutes get up and do something relaxing then go back to bed when you are tired.
2. **Take care of what you eat and drink** – don't go to bed hungry or 'bloated'. Over-indulging will cause discomfort and keep your body working. Too much drink will mean toilet visits in the night. Caffeine and nicotine are stimulants, and alcohol will disrupt your sleep.
3. **Have a bedtime routine** – a bath or shower, a book to read, calming music, lights dimmed will be good for some wind-down time. Television and computer screens are likely to be less restful.
4. **Set the scene** – make your environment conducive to slumber: cool, dark and quiet. Have a bed that suits you, a mattress and pillows that you choose personally. If you share the bed make sure it is big enough – make arrangements for any children and pets to have their own separate, comfort zones.
5. **Daytime nap** – make it short (less than 30 minutes) and make it mid-afternoon. If you work nights make your daytime sleep as much like a night-time routine as possible.
6. **Be active during the day** – regular physical exercise will induce deeper sleep, but be careful about late exercise as it can be a stimulant.

Reduce your stress – as much as possible get your world organised, set priorities, delegate what you can, take breaks, have fun, note anything you need to remember, put your mind at rest as much as possible before you retire.

Use the Mayo Clinic tips for a week and see how they work for you

16 http://www.mayoclinic.com/health/sleep/HQ01387

Life Enhancers
Activity 6: Find Life Enhancers

We all need treats from time-to-time to boost our spirits and help us move from more challenging, stressful times to gentler, happier ones. Could any of the following options be boosters for you when you need a restorative break?

Life Enhancer 1 - Have Fun

One suggestion, unproven, is that the average child laughs up to 300 times a day while the average adult laughs less than 20 times a day. The most miserable people apparently may raise a chuckle less than six times a day. Research-based or not, it is probably true that none of us laugh enough.

'There ain't much fun in medicine, but there is a heck of a lot of medicine in fun.' Josh Billings, American humourist

'The Art of medicine consists of keeping the patient amused while nature heals the disease.' Voltaire

'The simple truth is that happy people generally don't get sick.' Bernie Siegel, M.D.

The link between laughter and health is attracting attention in the medical world.[17]av At one stage the suggestion was that 85 per cent of all illnesses could be cured by the body's own healing system. Whether or not this is still the case, maintaining a happy and positive outlook on life is doubtless a very good way to support our well-being. Loving, joy, caring and laughing are always going to be better for us than hating, nagging, moaning and groaning.

Laughter, it is thought:
- builds relationships – we warm to people who make us laugh and who laugh with us, and laughter bonds us to each other – we laugh 30 times more in company than we ever do alone;
- becomes less a part of everyday life as we get older or become more senior at work;
- reduces stress and strengthens the body's immune system;
- exercises our heart – it raises our heartbeat and has been called 'internal jogging'. People with heart disease are 40 per cent less likely to laugh in a variety of situations than people of the same age without heart disease.
- helps us deal with conflicts and crises, relaxes muscles and reduces tension;
- indicates good self-esteem; a lack of a sense of humour has been linked to low self-esteem.

It is important to recognise that there is 'good' humour and 'bad' humour. Healthy humour
is where we laugh together, laugh at ourselves or our situations – it brings us together with others. 'Bad' humour is when it is at other people's expense, when it hurts and distances people from us. That type is not likely to be therapeutic or build happier lives.
So, laughter and fun are undoubtedly significant contributors to happiness and well-being. Where do we find what we need?

17 <http://www.helpguide.org/life/humor_laughter_health.htm>.

health and happiness

Why not try the following:

- Decide each day to look at the funny side of life and look for laughs in everyday situations.

- Spend time with fun friends or with children who can find fun in things much of the time.

- Watch or listen to funny programmes.

- Watch comedy films or shows.

- Look for cartoons and jokes in the daily papers or online.

- Remember a joke a day and tell it to others.

- Read humorous books.

- Watch and listen to comedians, go to comedy clubs.

- Don't spend too much time, if any, with grouches or pessimists.

- Avoid news bulletins that focus on life tragedies and disasters that we can do little about.

give these a try

- Do a fun review at intervals – ask yourself am I getting enough?

- So, on a scale of 1 to 10 (1 is 'Little' – 10 is 'Loads') how much fun and laughter is built into your life and work at present?

- Whatever your score is, it could probably be higher. What are you going to do about it?

- I will _____

_____

Some other resources:
- search the following terms on the internet: 'health and humour', 'fun and health', 'laughter and health', 'therapy and laughter', 'jokes'.

Life Enhancer 2 – Exercise Our Brain

We are aware that physical exercise is beneficial to our body and greatly enhances our general well-being. But what about the potential in mental exercise also? Key to our happier living is also the maintenance and health of our brain. We can look after our minds while we are looking after our bodies.

health and happiness

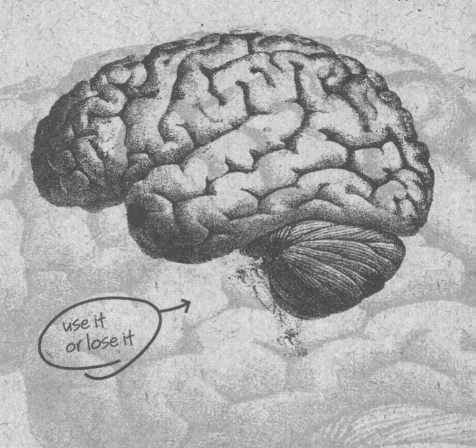

use it or lose it

'If we don't use it, we lose it!'[18]

The brain and the mind have the best chance of thriving and prospering if we keep them active. A study of 19,000 women aged between 70 and 81 published in the Journal of the American Medical Association indicated that those who had engaged in regular physical activity scored higher on a range of mental tests than those who were sedentary. Brain cells need oxygen just like every other cell in our body. So, a good healthy diet and an active life are the basic essentials of staying mentally alert.

18 <http://www.fi.edu/learn/brain/exercise.html#mentalexercise>.

Additionally, it's possible to keep mentally active by:
- doing crossword or sudoku puzzles, playing mentally challenging games and computer games;
- taking part in stimulating discussions, learning new skills, getting involved in further education;
- learning and playing a musical instrument;
- reading widely;
- going online;
- having an active social life, getting involved in local community groups;
- joining walking groups, dance classes, debating societies, political parties, political movements, pressure groups, women's groups, men's clubs, sports clubs;
- going to art or drama classes, listening to intelligent discussions or comedy on the radio, taking on new challenges, going to new places, watching plays and films;
- doing challenging voluntary work;
- teaching children things as they grow, playing games with them, reading them stories, telling them jokes
- having a purpose, an aim, a goal for each day, each week, each month;
- travelling, it can actually broaden the mind.

health and happiness

It's Never Too Late

Authors Terry Horne and Simon Wootton[19] and others urge us not to accept that our brain power is genetically determined and fixed for life. They claim we can continue to increase our brain's health and mental capacity by how we live and work. They maintain that diet, environment and lifestyle will impact on our brainpower.

They also recommend
- laughter;
- having friends with shared interests;
- avoiding negative people;
- and the pursuit of **BLISS** (**B**ody-based pleasure; **L**aughter; **I**nvolvement; **S**atisfaction; and **S**ex).

The claim is that all of these promote physical responses in us that benefit the health and well-being of our brains.

So, how do you plan to enhance your mental capacity and agility?

Visit these two websites and see what you think. They claim to offer free brain games:
www.braingle.com/brainteasers/index_tour.php
www.fi.edu/learn/brain/exercise.html#mentalexercise

Read this article to get an expert view on some myths about brain work:
www.guardian.co.uk/science/2008/nov/23/human-behaviour-science-dementia

Visit these websites

---

19 Terry Horne and Simon Wootton, Train Your Brain: Teach Yourself (Teach Yourself, 2010).

Life Enhancer 3 - Enjoy Culture

Recent research from the Norwegian University of Science and Technology has registered a link between cultural activities and health and happiness.[20] The research showed that:

- 'attending sporting events' was associated with good health in women and 'taking part in cultural activities' was good for men's health;
- taking part in creative activities increased women's life satisfaction and reduced the likelihood of them experiencing anxiety and depression;
- men could achieve the same benefits by 'observing' cultural events;
- the more involved both genders were in cultural life, the higher their reported physical health and mental well-being;
- leisure activities such as listening to music are good for stress reduction, while singing in choirs has the added bonus of increased social contacts and the improved mental health that results.

So, the message for all of us is that time spent in the pursuit of culture translates into better health and greater life satisfaction. How do we/can we get a cultural booster?

How many of these attract you now or might be worth exploring?
- Singing in a choir
- Going to the theatre, the ballet or the opera
- Playing an instrument or learning to do so
- Taking singing lessons
- Attending music festivals or concerts
- Going to poetry events
- Listening to music
- Visiting museums and art galleries
- Dancing

would you try these?

---

20 Reported by Martin Beckford, Health Correspondent in: 'Cultural activities good for men's health and happiness', The Telegraph, 23 May 2011, <http://www.telegraph.co.uk/health/healthnews/8530805/Cultural-activitiesgood-for-mens-health-and-happiness.html>.

health and happiness

- Playing a sport
- Attending sports events
- Joining a sports club
- Going to the cinema
- Joining walking groups
- Taking cultural holidays
- Going to historic buildings or heritage sites
- Joining a book club.

What is missing that you would add?

How active is your cultural life?
Very   Fairly   Not Very

How might you expand it to increase your health and happiness?

what would you add?

Life Enhancer 4 – Keep Committing to the Basics

Whatever you have taken from this section it would be good to finish by reminding ourselves of the basic messages of living healthily so we can make the most of our life.

We can't just read about it and get results. We have to **apply** our awareness.

All the research into the area is fascinating but the basic messages are consistent and universal. They are that if we want the best chance of living a long, fruitful and happy life, we should:

- not smoke;
- avoid alcohol abuse;
- enjoy good, stable relationships;
- do physical and mental exercise;
- eat healthily and maintain a healthy weight;
- avoid or manage stressful situations;
- meditate, pray, relax, do things that restore us;
- contribute to a cause, something we care about;
- continue learning;
- have fun and laugh more;
- be involved in social and productive activities;
- be positive and look for the good things in life;
- show gratitude;
- have regular medical checks;
- sleep well to restore body and mind;
- MAKE OTHERS HAPPY!

health and happiness

> Reflecting on your life at the moment:
>
> How many of the basics are part of your life now?
>
> Which might you wish to make some plans to work on?

There is a comprehensive health and lifestyle check on www.realage.com, which also produces lifestyle recommendations based on your score. The site is American, so a few questions may be more difficult to answer because of differences in medical terminology. Once you have signed up you will not only get your 'real age' assessment but regular health tips based on the latest research.

Other useful sites are:
- www.helpguide.org
- www.psychologytoday.com
- www.eatwell.gov.uk
- www.nutrition.org.uk
- www.bupa.co.uk
- www.diabetes.co.uk
- www.health.harvard.edu
- www.ageuk.org.uk
- www.workingforhealth.gov.uk

A Final Thought

A former BBC news presenter was once ridiculed for suggesting that there should be a 'good news' programme as the current pattern of news coverage presents all the negative, worrying, violent, tragic stories and little that is uplifting. Research is now suggesting that he might have been correct in that our constant diet of bad news stories really can invite depression. A US website set up to counter this can be found at: www.gimundo.com.

What Might You Want to Change?

You have had the opportunity to reflect on and find out more about healthier living as a basis for happier living.

On the basis of your reflections on your current health and well-being and the information you have surveyed in this section, write in what you would like more of, less of and what you would like to keep the same in your life right now. Reflect on your diet, exercise, sleep and life enhancers and plan any changes you would like to make.

health and happiness

More of	Less of	Keep the same

Choose three that you would like to start working on right now.
1.
2.
3.

you can start right now

Other life skills programmes on our website (livehappier.com) that you may want to consider to further explore Health and Happiness are:
- Focus on the Positive
- Avoid Perfectionism
- Be Optimistic
- Try the 'Wonder Drug'

live happier: the ultimate life skill

leisure

even if it doesn't always feel like it

Today, however, we have more discretionary time than we have ever had.

livehappier.com

Leisure and Happiness

What is Known About Leisure and Happiness?

Leisure, or free time, is usually defined as time spent away from business, work and domestic chores. It is also the periods of time before or after necessary activities such as eating, sleeping and, where it is compulsory, education.

We have always liked the distinction made by Jack Loughary and Theresa Ripley[1] between:

Sold Time – the time you get paid for, or if you are a student, the time you spend learning and studying (not playing!)

Maintenance Time – the time you spend on managing your life: sleeping, shopping, cooking, cleaning, eating, managing children or caring for others.

Discretionary Time – the time left that you can decide what to do with.

Do we have more or less leisure time today than in years gone by?

Marshall Sahlins in his fascinating book on Stone Age Economics[2] claims that men appeared to hunt from two to two-and-a-half days a week with an average working week of 15 hours. Women gathered food for about the same time. In fact, one day's work supplied a woman's family with vegetables for the next three days.

---

1   J. Loughary and T. Ripley, Second Chance: Everyone's Guide to Career Change (United Learning, 1975).
2   (Aldine Transaction, 1972).

The remainder of the time was for rest, playing games, gossiping, engaging in rituals and visiting one another.

The industrial revolution changed all of that. And what will be the impact of the digital revolution?

Today, however, we have more discretionary time than we have ever had – even if it doesn't always feel like that (especially with smart phones, tablets and computers).

Seven major factors have influenced the development of leisure and recreation during the twentieth century:
- increase in leisure time available to many individuals;
- increase in disposable income;
- improved mobility (e.g. car ownership, public transport systems);
- demographic changes (e.g. ageing population);
- changing fashions and trends;
- technological developments (home entertainment systems, computers);
- increased access to the countryside.

Men generally have more leisure time than women. In Europe and the United States, adult men usually have between one and nine hours more leisure time than women have each week.[3]

Research from Norwich and Peterborough Building Society shows that in a typical week, three in 10 adults spend over three hours online outside of work, with almost 7.5 million spending more than five hours of their own time online each day, or over 35 hours a week – the equivalent of a full-time job.

---

3   OECD (Organisation for Economic Cooperation and Development) (2009). Society at a Glance 2009: OECD Social Indicators, OECD publishing. p. 31. ISBN 92-64-04938-X. See image at http://dx.doi.org/10.1787/548724153767.

leisure and happiness

A survey by the Office for National Statistics in 2005 showed that an average of 142 minutes was spent on housework in Great Britain in 2005 – 30 minutes less than in 2000. Seventy-seven per cent of men and 92 per cent of women spent some time each day doing housework (compared with 86 per cent and 96 per cent respectively in 2000).

The three main activities carried out by people in Great Britain in 2011[4] were sleeping, working, and watching TV and videos/DVDs or listening to music. These activities take up more than half the day (13 hours and 38 minutes out of the 24 hours available). About one-third of the day was spent sleeping. Men were more likely to watch TV or listen to the radio and to take part in other activities (sport, entertainment, hobbies and using the computer). Women were more likely than men to spend time reading or with other people.

The distribution of activities varied during the week. At the weekend, both men and women spent more time sleeping and participating in leisure activities, and men spent more time on domestic work (161 minutes compared with 116 minutes on weekdays). The difference was due to more time being spent on repairs and gardening and shopping and appointments at the weekend.

Men have on average 30 minutes more free time per day than women although this is to some extent compensated for by the extra 20 minutes women spend sleeping on average. Less free time is enjoyed by men and women when there are children in the household. Men aged between 16 and 49 with children of pre-school age have 231 free minutes per day compared with 348 minutes for those without dependent children.

---

4 <http://www.culture.gov.uk/publications/8398.aspx>.

But Don't Holidays Make Us Happy?

The simple answer would appear to be – a bit – but not for very long. More research is being conducted by psychologists into this issue. Following considerable research, Jeroen Nawijn from NHTV Breda University in The Netherlands has proposed a 'holiday happiness curve'. During the first 10 per cent of a holiday people are generally in lower mood (he calls this the 'travel phase'); those between 10 per cent and 80 per cent of the trip (the 'core phase') are in high mood; those between 80 and 90 per cent of the trip are in the 'decline phase'; and those in the final 10 per cent (the 'rejuvenation phase') find that a higher mood prevails. Nawijn believes this last phase is where people have left behind their worries about packing and the frustration of the trip coming to an end. They are able to enjoy the trip again and possibly also look forward to going home.

Other studies show a small but significant positive effect on well-being following a holiday. However, this disappears within two to four weeks of being home. A study of thousands of men with heart disease showed that the more holidays they took the more likely they were to survive the study's nine-year follow-up period.

Interestingly, the most strongly recalled incidences of happiness on holidays were associated with the most memorable or unusual 24-hour period of the holiday. One implication, say the researchers, is that if you want to have a memorable holiday then it helps to include one experience that is likely to be memorable rather than simply lying on the same beach all day, every day.

leisure and happiness

Life Skill: Understand How You Spend Your Time

It is always useful to analyse just how you do spend your time.

Activity 1: How Do You Spend Your Time?

It is not unusual for people to spend huge amounts of time analysing returns and pay-offs from investments, working out the 'best buy' for a freezer, DVD or mobile phone, or spending hours bidding on eBay, yet we quite often fail to transfer these considerable analytical skills to our own lives.

It can be valuable to reflect regularly on:
- What returns am I getting for the time and energy I am investing?
- What parts of my life are 'best buys'?
- How am I actually filling the hours of each day?
- What would it be good to change?

We know from research into weight control that most of us are notoriously unreliable when it comes to recalling what we eat and the same is true for how we spend our time. Consequently, we invite you to keep a record of your activities for what you think is a fairly typical week of your life.

It is best done by recording what you have done at the end of each day. You can print it out and fill it in by hand or, to give you more space, create your own.

My Time Investment Record

	am	pm
Monday		
Tuesday		
Wednesday		
Thursday		

leisure and happiness

Friday		
Saturday		
Sunday		

After you have completed your time log for a week please fill in your responses to the following questions:

Is this a typical week?

What does this snapshot tell me about the way I am spending my time?

How much of my week was spent doing things I chose to do?

What might I want to change?

_____

_____

_____

What are the most rewarding things I do that I would like to do more of?

_____

_____

_____

What are the least rewarding things that I would like to do less of?

_____

_____

leisure and happiness

Activity 2: Sold, Maintenance and Discretionary Time

Look again at your Time Investment Record. Use three different coloured pens, one for each of the three categories and colour in each entry according to whether you think it is sold, maintenance or discretionary time. What proportion do you have for each?

Now make a list of your activities in each of the three categories using labels that make sense to you.

Take a large sheet of paper and write down the activities under each heading on the left-hand side and write in the hours spent during each day of the week

Maintenance	1	2	3	4	5	6	7	8	9	10
Sleeping										
Eating										
Cleaning										
Washing										
Make up										
Shopping										
etc										

fill this table in

Sold	1	2	3	4	5	6	7	8	9	10
At work										
Commuting										
Working at home										
Studying										
etc										

Discretionary	1	2	3	4	5	6	7	8	9	10
With partner										
Watching TV										
On computer										
Gym										
etc										

What does this tell you about how you are investing your time right now?

Does it highlight any changes that you would like to make?

Are you making the most of your discretionary (leisure) time?

leisure and happiness

Life Skill: Know Your Interests
Activity 3: What Leisure Interests Should I Pursue?

Your interests represent your preferences for doing some activities rather than others. Some people like cooking, others like driving cars, some like blogging, and others like to paint or read books or do voluntary work.

Psychologists have suggested that people's interests incline them to particular types of work. People in the same occupation, although they may have different values are likely to have similar skills and interests.

Below are six sets of statements. For each of them, show how much you agree or disagree with the statement by circling a number from 1 to 5.

 = Highly disagree    = Highly agree

Interests – Group P (these intials are explained later)

I like fixing and repairing things	1	2	3	4	5
I like to keep fit	1	2	3	4	5
I like making things with my hands	1	2	3	4	5
I like doing things outdoors	1	2	3	4	5
I like hard, physical work	1	2	3	4	5
I enjoy working with tools and machines	1	2	3	4	5

Add up the numbers
Total for P =

Interests – Group FI

I like to understand things thoroughly	1	2	3	4	5
I like exploring new ideas	1	2	3	4	5
I enjoy working on problems	1	2	3	4	5
I like asking questions	1	2	3	4	5

leisure and happiness

I like learning about new things   1 2 3 4 5
I like to work out my own answers
to problems   1 2 3 4 5

Add up the numbers

Total for FI =

Interests Group A

I like seeing art shows, plays and
good films   1 2 3 4 5
I like to be different   1 2 3 4 5
I forget about everything else when   1 2 3 4 5
I'm being creative   1 2 3 4 5
It is vital to have beautiful and unusual
things around me   1 2 3 4 5
I like to use my imagination   1 2 3 4 5
I like expressing myself through
writing, painting or music   1 2 3 4 5

Add up the numbers

Total for A =

Interests Group S

I enjoy being with people	1	2	3	4	5
I like to talk things through with people	1	2	3	4	5
I like to pay attention to what people want	1	2	3	4	5
I like helping people	1	2	3	4	5
I like helping people develop and learn things	1	2	3	4	5
Who I am with is more important than where I am	1	2	3	4	5

Add up the numbers

Total for S =

Interests Group E

I enjoy trying to persuade and influence people	1	2	3	4	5
I enjoy using a great deal of energy	1	2	3	4	5
I like people to do what I ask of them	1	2	3	4	5
I like taking risks	1	2	3	4	5
I like making decisions	1	2	3	4	5
I enjoy getting people organised and excited about doing a task	1	2	3	4	5

Add up the numbers

Total for E =

leisure and happiness

Interests Group R

I like to be given clear directions	1	2	3	4	5
I enjoy getting the details right in my work	1	2	3	4	5
I like a clear structure and regular routine	1	2	3	4	5
I can be relied upon to do what I'm expected to do	1	2	3	4	5
I enjoy working with figures	1	2	3	4	5
I like organising projects, ideas and people down to the last detail	1	2	3	4	5

Add up the numbers

Total for R =

Rank order the letters P/FI/A/S/E/R according to the interest group in which you have the highest and lowest scores.

P   FI   A

S   E   R

The descriptions of what these letters mean are on the next page.

Practical Interests: P
Your high score in PRACTICAL interests indicates you like to work with tools, objects, machines and animals. Your score indicates that you like to develop manual, mechanical, agricultural and electronic skills. You like building and repairing things, and you like to work with your hands. You admire physical coordination, strength, agility and logic, and like to work outdoors and deal with specific problems. Finally, you prefer to solve problems by DOING.

Finding Out Interests: F
Your high score in FINDING OUT interests indicates a preference for activities with an investigative focus. You like to use your brain. You are likely to be curious, studious, independent and sometimes unconventional. You like to develop skills in mathematics, biology and physical sciences, and prefer jobs with a scientific or medical focus. You admire logic, use insight, enjoy intellectual challenge. You enjoy solving problems by THINKING them through.

Artistic Interests: A
Your high score in ARTISTIC interests indicates a preference for activities with an artistic focus. If you score high in this group of interests, language, art, music, drama and writing hold some importance and you tend to be creative, expressive and somewhat independent. You like to be free from routine. You can be non-conformist, sensitive and introspective. You enjoy being CREATIVE when you solve problems.

Social Interests: S
Your high score in SOCIAL interests indicates that activities with a people focus are likely to be of interest to you. You like activities that involve informing, training, teaching, understanding and helping others. You tend to develop skills for helping others such as those needed by teachers, nurses and counsellors. Because you tend to be helpful, friendly, sensitive, supportive, genuine and empathetic, you like to solve problems by using your FEELINGS.

Enterprising Interests: E
Your high score in ENTERPRISING interests indicates that activities

involving people and data are likely to be of interest to you. You enjoy leading and influencing people, and are often outgoing, ambitious, independent, enthusiastic and logical. You like projects. You enjoy organising, getting people to work as a team, managing, variety, status, power and money. You like to lead, motivate and persuade people. You typically solve problems by taking RISKS.

Routine Interests: R
Your high score in ROUTINE interests indicates you have a preference for order and clearly defined routines. You have an eye for detail. You like order, security and certainty, often identifying with power and status. You probably like developing work systems and utilising new technology. You like organising information in a clear and logical way, and you tend to be careful, logical, dependable and accurate, and solve problems by following ROUTINES.

Ask yourself the following questions:

Am I surprised at my interest scores? In what way?

What leisure activities might satisfy someone with my interests?

ask yourself

Life Skill: Match Your Leisure To Your Interests

If you have not done so already complete the Life Skill: Knowing Your Interests.
Are they: artistic, enterprising, social, practical, finding out or routine?.

Opposite are lists of leisure interests that fit for each of the main interest areas. These lists suggest activities that might more closely match your interests. It does not imply that you will have the necessary skills, only the motivation.

leisure and happiness

Practical interests – possible leisure links

- Repairing or mending things
- Bike or horse riding
- Walking, hiking, running
- Camping, caravanning
- Playing football, cricket, hockey, netball
- Making things like model aircraft, dresses, etc., using patterns or instruction kits
- Cooking
- Car or bike racing
- Gardening, allotments
- DIY
- Mountain climbing
- Ice-skating, roller skating
- Aerobic dancing, fitness classes
- Skiing
- Skin diving/scuba diving
- Working out in a gym
- Jogging alone
- Swimming
- Archery
- Training animals
- Hang-gliding, sky diving
- Carpentry
- Candle making
- Winemaking
- Sewing
- Bee keeping
- Restoring cars, furniture, houses.

Finding out interests – possible leisure links

- Developing and processing photos
- Reading books and magazines on scientific or technical subjects
- Observing, collecting, identifying such things as birds, animals, plants, fossils, shells, rocks, etc.
- Visiting museums, scientific or technical displays
- Watching and listening to documentaries or 'in-depth" reports on TV, radio or the internet
- Playing chess, draughts, bridge, scrabble, mastermind, or other games of skill and mental agility
- Computer programming
- Research involving the internet
- Genealogy
- Self-development
- Alternative therapies
- Meditation
- Attending lectures
- Various adult education courses.

Social interests – possible leisure links

- Visiting and working with the less able, older people, etc.
- Taking part in guides, scouts, youth groups, church and religious groups
- Planning and giving parties
- Running or walking with others
- Raising funds for charities
- Working with young children in play groups, Sunday schools, cubs, brownies, etc.
- Activities with family
- Playing games or sport with friends or family
- Spending social time with friends or colleagues at pubs, dinner parties, restaurants
- Massage or martial arts (or possibly both though not at once!)
- Joining clubs or activities primarily for the social functions
- Using the computer for social contacts and networking, e.g. Facebook, Twitter, Myspace, etc.
- Travelling with friends or a group
- Playing games where winning is not the most important thing
- Playing computer games which need other players
- Belonging to virtual communities like Second Life
- Shopping with friends

Artistic interests – possible leisure links

- Learning or playing a musical instrument or singing
- Writing short stories or poetry
- Sketching, drawing or painting
- Taking part in plays or musicals
- Designing websites or new computer games
- Craftwork, e.g. pottery, weaving, knitting, jewellery-making, macramé, etc.
- Visiting art galleries and exhibitions
- Going to the cinema, plays or concerts
- Flower arranging
- Yoga
- Photography
- Gem polishing
- Dancing
- Interior decorating
- Restoring antiques
- Sculpting
- Visiting National Trust properties and gardens, or similar
- Singing.

leisure and happiness

Enterprising interests – possible leisure links

- Playing monopoly, backgammon, poker, or other games of chance
- Doing small jobs, such as gardening or car cleaning or repairs for a fee
- Taking part in debates or making speeches
- Starting a debating group
- Following politics in the newspaper, or on radio, TV or internet

- Managing a committee
- Earning money by selling things
- Car boot sales
- Games where winning is important
- Making homebrew beer or wine to save money
- Entering craftwork in competitions
- Promoting charities or fundraising.

possible leisure links

Routine interests – possible leisure links

- Using calculators or computers for record-keeping
- Keeping detailed accounts or a careful diary
- Tidying up sheds, cupboards, drawers, etc.
- Keeping times and recording results at sporting events

- Collecting and cataloguing coins, stamps, photo albums, scrap books Calligraphy
- Designing timetables for social events.

Activity 5: My Favourite Leisure Time Activities

From the list of possible leisure activities now pick your 10 favourite ones. If your favourite is not in the list just add it.

Think carefully about them and now rank order them from 1 to 10 with 1 being your favourite.

Include any that you would like to try but have not yet got around to doing.

Each of the columns asks you a question about that activity. Write in the letter or symbol suggested to build up a picture of how you are using your leisure time or would ideally like to spend it.

leisure and happiness

Leisure activity	Alone (a) or with people (p)	It costs £10 or more (£)	Does it involve risk? Physical (p) Intellectual (i) Emotional (e)	Energetic (e) Non-energetic (ne)	Do you do it Often (o) Sometimes (s) Rarely (r) Never (n)	When did you last do it?
1.						
2.						
3.						
4.						
5.						
6.						
7.						
8.						
9.						
10.						

From working with people using these exercises here are some examples of what people discovered.

One person discovered that he needed a balance between 'doing things with others' and 'doing things alone' and that he was not spending enough time doing things alone.

Another person was not surprised to find a high level of physical risk in her interests but realised she was not making enough time for them.

One person found that he was doing hardly any of the things that he really enjoyed.

One person realised that her favourite activities cost her almost nothing and her partner found three activities from the previous exercise that he had never thought of doing but now had included in his list.

Interestingly, another person, a very successful store manager (Enterprising) realised that he did not want leisure pursuits that were driven by that interest. Instead as a contrast he liked to experiment with digital photography (Artistic).

What do your entries say about your leisure?

leisure and happiness

To find out more...

Ask your friends if any of them engage in any leisure activities not included in the lists.

What might you want to change?

On the basis of your reflections on your current leisure profile and the alternatives you have surveyed in this section write in what you would like more of, less of and what you would like to keep the same in your leisure life right now.

More of	Less of	Keep the same

Choose three that you would like to start working on right now.

1.
2.
3.

live happier: the ultimate life skill

learning

what motivates your learning?

This chapter is designed to give you more insight into:
- how you learn and what motivates you to continue learning;
- the way you personally learn – your preferred learning style;
- the different learning methods that are available to you.

Learning and Happiness

What is Known About Learning and Happiness?

Most people like learning new things. If we wish to avoid rusting away or becoming increasingly out of touch or left behind then we need to continue learning for the rest of our lives.

Sadly, some people are put off learning because of unfortunate experiences at school. But, it is vitally important to remember that we were very young then, possibly badly taught, and this was only 'formal' learning. It has been estimated[1] that up to 90 per cent of everything we learn is learnt outside of schools, colleges and training courses.

The research also tells us of the very strong links between learning new things and feeling happy.

So, ask yourself what have you learnt which is new to you:

Today?

In the past week?

In the past month?

---

1   S. Merriam, R. Caffarella and L. Baumgartner, Learning in Adulthood: A Comprehensive Guide (3rd ed.)(Wiley, New York, 2007).

How many of these things have you learnt formally and how many have you learnt by yourself, from being with friends or colleagues or from the media (TV, papers, radio, magazines, internet, etc.)?

Many people planning for the future have learning high on their agenda. It could be learning about different places, different cultures, a new sport or hobby, new skills. It could be about developing new interests – genealogy, photography, working an allotment, working for a charity or community group.

This chapter is designed to give you more insight into:
- how you learn and what motivates you to continue learning;
- the way you personally learn – your preferred learning style;
- the different learning methods that are available to you.

It will help you to understand and develop the skills you need to improve your own learning and performance.

Being a Successful Learner

This is a question that a great deal of research has tried to answer. Why is it that sometimes the learning we undertake fails dramatically, while other times we succeed? There are several answers to this question but all of them contain one element in common – motivation!

Our attitude to our own learning is all-important. If we don't take charge of our own development, no one else will! Therefore, it's vital that we are motivated and willing to learn.

learning and happiness

Become a Motivated Learner

Research suggests that the following factors need to be in place if learning is to be successful:

- Access and opportunity – you need to be able to tap into the sources and resources appropriate to what you want to learn. These may be formal or informal, tutor-led or self-directed.
- Information and guidance – you need to be clear about what you want to learn, and have the support and guidance you need to learn it.
- Purpose – be clear what you want to get out of or achieve from your learning. Have goals to aim for.
- Relevance – it will help to recognise why the learning is important, how you will use it in your career or your life.
- Affordable – this doesn't mean simply financially affordable, but affordable in terms of time, resources, etc.
- Rewarded and celebrated – we all need recognition for our achievements, whether it is in the form of qualification, monetary reward or simply positive feedback; without it our motivation may slip.

Each of these elements is important, and a failure to learn in the past can often be traced back to a problem in one of these areas. Think of some learning you've sought or undertaken in your life that did not work out; perhaps a course you didn't complete, or a subject you weren't good at at school. Were any of the above factors missing?

Motivation comes when we are committed to doing something. When we can see it makes sense. When we can see a return for our efforts. When we want it badly. 'Ownership' is a key word in learning and development. When you 'own' your own development, when you take responsibility for achieving things and are keen to progress, when you choose to work at it, when you are hungry for the benefits it can bring, you are highly likely to succeed. Each of us will work hard at the things we value and for which we can see 'pay-offs'. Pay-offs are not necessarily material gains; they could be greater self-confidence and self-satisfaction, a sense of achievement or new status.

Why is it important to go on learning as we get older?

Learning:
- keeps our mind sharp;
- improves memory and helps keep our brain smart and active;
- increases self-confidence and optimism;
- can maintain our sense of 'advancement' rather than 'decline';
- offers an inexpensive way to try something new;
- can save us money as we learn to 'do it ourselves';
- gives us a feeling of accomplishment;
- helps us meet people who share our interests;
- can add to our social life and build new contacts;
- builds on skills we already have;
- offers us an opportunity to learn a new skill or trade and increase our income;
- gives us a new interest that we can share with family and friends...

...and can actually be fun!

learning can be fun

Life Skill: Know How You Learn

Activity 1: What is My Learning Style?

We have talked about the theory of how people learn and what motivates them to continue learning. But, how do you personally learn? We are all individuals, and every one of us has our own personal style or way of learning.

The following activity will help you identify and think about your own learning style. It will also help you to understand how you learn best, and will show you ways in which your style may differ from other people's styles.

Before you complete this questionnaire it is important to know that each learning style has its advantages and disadvantages. There is no 'best' style – all of them are equally valid – each has its strengths and shortfalls.

For each of the following statements, decide whether the statement is:

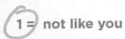   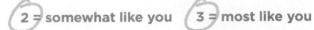

Circle the option that you think best describes you. (Ignore the letters in the brackets)

1.	I work systematically on those subjects I don't enjoy, as well as on those I do. [L]	1 2 3
2.	I check through everything I write to ensure its flow and accuracy. [L]	1 2 3
3.	I pay great attention to detail in all I do. [L]	1 2 3
4.	I like to understand how things work and how ideas have been developed. [L]	1 2 3
5.	I enjoy solving problems and posing new questions. [L]	1 2 3

learning and happiness

6. I like finishing one task before undertaking another. [L] 1 2 3

7. I am a good critic, asking searching questions and raising doubts. [L] 1 2 3

8. I prefer to work through problems for myself. [L] 1 2 3

9. I like to make lists, work out timetables and have clear action plans. [L] 1 2 3

10. I prefer to listen to ideas rather than talk. [L] 1 2 3

11. I re-work any project until I get it absolutely right. [L] 1 2 3

12. I stick to timetables and action plans I have made. [L] 1 2 3

13. I learn best by studying things for myself. [L] 1 2 3

14. I like reading for ideas and coming to my own conclusions. [L]

15.	I am intuitive rather than methodical in my work. [1]	1 2 3
16.	I like to spend a lot of time just thinking. [1]	1 2 3
17.	I like making connections between different topics, enjoying seeing how ideas link together. [1]	1 2 3
18.	I can spend a long time thinking about work without actually getting down to it. [1]	1 2 3
19.	I prefer thinking and talking to written assignments. [1]	1 2 3
20.	I like to find original, new ways of completing and presenting work. [1]	1 2 3
21.	I like to work in bursts of energy. [1]	1 2 3
22.	I like to float ideas around with other people. [1]	1 2 3

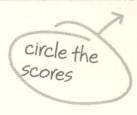

circle the scores

learning and happiness

23. I am comfortable working without timetables or plans. [I]   1 2 3

24. I enjoy coming up with new questions and alternatives. [I]   1 2 3

25. I would rather work from, and produce, creative diagrams than straightforward lists. [I]   1 2 3

26. I don't like detail, I prefer seeing the whole picture. [I]   1 2 3

27. I enjoy challenging ideas. [I]   1 2 3

28. I like daydreaming, for me it's fruitful. [I]   1 2 3

29. I like a clear purpose and direction. [P]   1   2   3

30. I like planning my work. [P]   1   2   3

31. I like to know exactly what is required or expected before starting a project. [P]   1   2   3

32. I know what is important to me and what I want to achieve. [P]   1   2   3

33. I like working on my own. [P]   1   2   3

34. I like to get on with a task and not be side-tracked by new approaches to life. [P]   1   2   3

35. I respect deadlines and am impatient with those who don't. [P]   1   2   3

36. I am usually very well organised. [P]   1   2   3

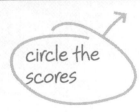
circle the scores

learning and happiness

37. I think in advance about equipment and resources I need for work. [P]   1 2 3

38. I use lists, charts and graphs that give data rather than attempt to produce works of art. [P]   1 2 3

39. I enjoy getting down to work. [P]   1 2 3

40. I read instructions carefully and work methodically, I like timetables and agendas. [P]   1 2 3

41. I enjoy finishing a task. [P]   1 2 3

circle the scores

42. I get bored easily and enjoy moving on to new things. [E]	1 2 3
43. I enjoy working in groups. [E]	1 2 3
44. I am not interested in detail. [E]	1 2 3
45. I learn by talking through ideas with other people. [E]	1 2 3
46. I like getting on with things; doing is more attractive than planning. [E]	1 2 3
47. I like variety; I like flitting from one task to another. [E]	1 2 3
48. When I'm interested I get totally involved, when I'm not I shy away from topics. [E]	1 2 3
49. I like skip reading; trying to absorb everything is not my style. [E]	1 2 3

learning and happiness

50. I enjoy writing freely, letting the ideas flow rather than thinking things through first. [E]   1   2   3

51. I don't read through or check my work once it's completed. [E]   1   2   3

52. I like asking lots of questions to find out all I need to know. [E]   1   2   3

53. I like new ideas and approaches. [E]   1   2   3

54. I like to take life as it comes and be spontaneous. [E]   1   2   3

You will have noticed that each statement has one of the letters L, I, P or E in brackets.

Calculate your score by adding up the scores for L, I, P and E.

You scored _____ as a Logical learner (L)

You scored _____ as an Imaginative learner (I)

You scored _____ as a Practical learner (P)

You scored _____ as an Enthusiastic learner (E)

Your highest score indicates your dominant learning style – the one that has got you the best learning results in your life so far. We each have the capacity to extend our learning style but over the years we tend to stick to what works best for us.

Remember, there is no one 'best' style – each style has its advantages and disadvantages.

On the next page, you will find a description of the characteristics of each style of learning. Look at your scores and then check out the descriptions that follows. Do these descriptions mirror the ways in which you choose to learn or not choose to learn?

remember this

learning and happiness

Logical Learners

Advantages	Disadvantages
Organise work well	Can need too much information and over-elaborate
Are keen to understand things and make links	Can get bogged down in the theory
Are curious; keen to learn; enjoy problems	Can be reluctant to try new approaches
Plan well, and work systematically	Can be set in their ways and uncreative
Are precise and thorough	Tend not to use others as support
Like debate, are good critics	Tend not to be adventurous
Will rework things and iron out errors	Work from the head rather than the heart
	Trust only logic

Imaginative Learners

Advantages	Disadvantages
Are able to see new ways of working	Are not attracted to detail; like to see the 'big picture'
Produce creative solutions	Can be slow to actually get down to work
Can see long-term implications and consequences	Can be uncritical of ideas
Are unhurried; tend to be easygoing and unflappable	Can be too easygoing and unassertive
Listen to others and share ideas	Tend to work in bursts of energy, rather than systematically
See links between topics and concepts	Can be somewhat disorganised
Will work in novel and artistic ways	
Are able to pinpoint important questions	

Practical Learners

Advantages	Disadvantages
Work well on their own	Expect others to be clear and thorough; can be impatient with those who are not
Are good at setting goals and making action plans	
Know how to find out what they need to know	Believe own way is the best and only right way
Are good at applying theories	Tend not to use others for support
Get things done on time	Can be preoccupied with the details and fail to see the 'big picture'
Are single-minded, not easily distracted	
Are organised, and good time managers	Can lack imagination
Are thorough; absorb information well	Can be more interested in the completion, than the quality of work
Have organised filing/retrieval systems	

Enthusiastic Learners

Advantages	Disadvantages
Will throw themselves into things that interest them	May not be keen on planning and organising
Will work well with others; likely to use and give support	Can be difficult to motivate when the topic does not interest them
Will try new ideas	Likely to take on too many things at once
Work quickly and get others enthusiastic	Not likely to rework what they produce, will be keen to move on to the next topic
Enjoy variety and excitement	
Will question and challenge; enjoy talking about ideas	Likely to work to priorities and to leave things to the last minute
Like skip reading or writing freely	Can have difficulty in focusing

learning and happiness

Remember:
- We often expect others to learn in the same way as ourselves. Our style works for us, but different styles work for different people. 'Logicals' are likely to have the most difficulty when working with 'Enthusiasts' and vice versa. 'Practicals' and 'Imaginatives' may not feel comfortable when starting to work with each other.
- We all have the capacity to develop the other styles, our dominant one is simply the one that we have used most so far, and which we find most suitable.
- We need to understand the features of different styles so we can work with other people in a style that makes sense to them. When we can work in other styles, people feel that we are on their 'wavelength', and if we are part of a team the team will be able to work more effectively.
- If you are working through this programme with a buddy you may find that person learns in a different way to you. If you understand this then there can be real advantages in working with someone with a different style as they will bring a different slant to a task, which could be illuminating. On the other hand it could be frustrating! Work with them because with patience you may learn something to your advantage.

These learning styles also have implications when you decide which is the best learning method for you

Learning Methods

It's important to realise that there are many methods of learning available to us, and if we have an understanding of which method suits us best, our learning will be far more successful.

Below, you will find a variety of learning methods. As you read through these think about the methods which work best for you.

Coaching
Coaching allows people to develop skills in a controlled, yet flexible, environment. It is not about being 'taught', but about being helped to learn through experience. This type of learning draws on the experience of the coach to guide and assist the learner through the problems and pitfalls of a task in a real situation. He or she will also help the learner to review tasks to improve future performance.

Mentoring
A mentor is an experienced and trusted adviser. They can be a manager, a colleague, or any skilled and experienced person. A mentor can give useful advice and insights, and can also set informal development tasks to improve our knowledge or skills. A learner and a mentor will, over time, build a relationship based on trust and focused on our development.

Shadowing
One of the most popular and traditional methods of learning is to observe or shadow someone who is an expert while he or she works. As long as the learning is monitored, and reviews and standards are applied, this can be a very useful way of learning specific skills.

Courses
This is the most traditional way of learning, by being led by a specialist in a particular topic. There are many different traditional education and training courses available to you. The internet increasingly offers masses of learning opportunities, many of them free and some of them from recognised universities.

Networking
Networking is about making and maintaining effective contacts. This encourages you to consider and involve others in your learning activities. For example, by lending someone a copy of a report, sending them a website reference or by passing on some useful tips, you can then expect to receive similar support yourself.

Group or Team Sessions
This is an effective way of learning that offers excellent opportunities for team-building and team development. It is also a great way of learning from other people and sharing your own expertise.

Flexible/Open/eLearning
This involves working through a programme alone, much like you are on this one. The great advantage of this approach is that it allows you to be self-motivating and self-managing. It also allows you to study where, when, and in the way you choose. Depending on your style you could also feel quite isolated.

Which of the above sources or methods of learning will best suit your learning style?

which suits you?

What do you see as your next learning requirements in terms of your career or your life?

What do you need to do to make this happen?

Activity 2: Which Learning Method is Best for You?

Look at the table on the next page and decide which learning method you think suits you best. Remember, the ideas above are only suggestions. There is no right or wrong way to learn and you shouldn't be put off from learning in any way you wish. For the most complete learning experience, you should try a mixture of different learning methods. Mastering new ways of learning will broaden your abilities and help you accelerate your development.

The table links learning methods with learning styles.

	Logicals	Imaginatives	Practicals	Enthusiasts
Coaching	Like to have time to absorb things and ask detailed questions at his or her own pace.	Like to have an opportunity to really talk through things in a relaxed way.	Like direct help and full attention, without waiting for others to catch up.	Benefit from a structured approach to learning and having to demonstrate understanding or competence.
Mentoring	Like an opportunity to talk through things in detail and without pressure.	Like to talk through things in an unhurried way and to bounce ideas off colleagues.	Benefit from talking through ideas and plans when receiving feedback.	Benefit from formulating ideas and then explaining them to other people to receive feedback.
Shadowing	Like to analyse in detail and good at observation. Benefit from doing something that is real and not theoretical.	Would benefit from watching real behaviour.	Like an action-based, hands on approach to learning.	Like to learn from activity.

	Logicals	Imaginatives	Practicals	Enthusiasts
Courses	Like to learn from systematic training but dislike ambiguous situations.	Would benefit from listening to views from a wider group but dislike large groups.	Like to learn only if it is relevant. Would benefit from taking a different perspective.	Like to learn in large groups.
Networking	Like to develop systems but would benefit from having to make them happen.	Like to set up supportive relationships and enjoy helping others.	Like to develop their own contacts for mutual benefit.	Like to make new relationships and to have a wide circle of colleagues.
Group or Team Sessions	Would benefit from listening to others and working as part of a team.	Like to talk and listen in a team about ideas and concepts. Like to be creative.	Would benefit from working with team members.	Like to learn by talking with others but would benefit from having assignments agreed by the team.
Flexible/ Open/ eLearning	Like to work at own pace and to work thoroughly.	Like to have time to reflect without being pressurised to complete a task.	Like to work on their own without the distractions of working with others.	Would benefit from taking time to think things through for themselves.

Whichever style and method best supports our learning, its success will be limited unless we can learn from our mistakes.

learning and happiness

One of the most important stages in the learning process is reviewing the learning experience. Taking time to do this will ensure we stay on target. Often the best source of review can come from the people around us, who can give us their perspective on how we are doing.

It would be especially useful for you to learn with a buddy to enable you to compare learning styles and to explore with them the implications for learning.

What might you want to change?

Review the information and your answers about Learning.

Now complete the table on the following page by writing in what you want more of, less of and what you would like to keep the same in your life right now.

	More of	Less of	Keep the same
Learning styles			
Learning methods			

Choose three that you would like to start working on right now:
1.
2.
3.

you can start right now

learning and happiness

live happier: the ultimate life skill

home

we can learn a lot from the japanese

If living happier leads to longer lives then we have much to learn from the Japanese. Research into the lifestyle of the world's longest living community on the island of Okinawa suggests that it is not just a focus on diet and exercise that produces so many active, happy centenarians, but rather creating the right holistic surroundings.

Home and Happiness

What is Known About the Location of Our Home and Happiness?

Does where we live make any difference to our happiness? There are, in fact, regular research projects to identify which countries are the happiest in the world and in some cases which parts of which countries are the happiest places to live.[1] There is also much known about the features of the places that give those who live there the greatest likelihood of living long and happier lives.

The Happiest Countries

Using data produced in extensive research projects by Gallup and others, sociologist Dr Ruut Veenhoven and a Dutch team of colleagues have compiled the *World Database of Happiness*.[2] Another group of researchers from the University of Leicester have carried out a similar exercise and produced the *World Map of Happiness*.[3] A third project, the Happy Planet Index[4] rates international levels of happiness when balanced against the environmental impact a country makes.

All three projects place Costa Rica, in Central America, as the happiest place on earth, with the first two also making Denmark a very close second.

What are the features of these two very different countries that make their populations so satisfied with their lives?

---

1 See <http://mapscroll.blogspot.com/2010/03/mapping-global-happiness.html and/or http://www.mapsofworld.com/world-maps/happiness.html and/or http://www.wikiprogress.org/index.php/Happy_Planet_Index>.
2 <www.nytimes.com/2010/01/07/opinion/07kristof>.
3 <http://www.mapsofworld.com/world-maps/happiness.html>.
4 <http://www.happyplanetindex.org/public-data/files/happy-planet-index-2-0.pdf>.

Observers assessing a happy Costa Rica point to:
- a population who enjoy contented, happy lives and good longevity, lived in a sustainable economy, sensitive to nature;
- a wonderful climate in a beautiful country with glorious beaches, with the environment treated as an economic asset;
- a government that abolished its armed forces in 1949 and invested the money saved in the education and development of its people;
- an educated, stable, harmonious society, at peace with itself;
- rising levels of education that achieve significant gender equality (ahead of the USA) benefit economic productivity and attract tourism;
- progress in education leading to improvements in health care;
- ecological awareness and progress that compares well with European standards;
- a Latin-American culture that places high value on family and friends, cooperation and community.

observers point to

Denmark is a vastly different country, colder, in northern Europe, but has a very happy population despite having to pay between 50 per cent and 70 per cent of their income in taxation.[5]

Observers put Danish happiness down to:
- having a small population and an egalitarian culture with low reward differentials, meaning people tend not to choose careers based on status or salary;

---

5 Bill Weir, Denmark: The Happiest Place on Earth <http://abcnews.go.com/GMA/video/happy-movedenmark-2255811>.

home and happiness

- the Government paying for all education and health care and spending more per capita on children and older people than any other country in the world;
- a population who feel '*tryghed*' (Danish for 'tucked in'/'made snug') by its Government;
- having low differentials in earnings; artists can earn as much as refuse collectors or carpenters, who can earn as much as doctors; there being no class system (the Danes have a saying about '*jante-lov*' meaning nobody is better than anybody else);
- mixed neighbourhoods housing people from all walks of life;
- a very sociable culture; people enjoy spending time with friends and family and in spontaneous social gatherings (called '*hygge*');
- 92 per cent of Danes belonging to a social club who meet to sing or dance or share a hobby and these clubs are paid for by the Government;
- the Danes seeing their society as 'post-consumerist' – they love stylish things but are not obsessed by shopping and spending;
- valuing social time and activity more than 'stuff';
- having a very high level of trust in each other, in society and in their Government (happiness and trust levels are highly correlated) ('trust boxes' on unattended market stalls, children left in pushchairs while parents shop inside, unlocked bicycles are all common sights that indicate social trust);
- the bicycle being extremely popular, registering the Danish attachment to green values, to healthy living, to no need for status; and
- Denmark having one of the lowest unemployment rates in Europe.

a sociable culture

A Long and Happy Life

If living happier leads to longer lives then we have much to learn from the Japanese. Research[6] into the lifestyle of the world's longest living community on the island of Okinawa suggests that it is not just a focus on diet and exercise that produces so many active, happy centenarians, but rather creating the right holistic surroundings.

We can learn from them that we will have longer, happier lives if we:
- live in habitats which invite and require a good deal of walking – to neighbours, to shops, to community facilities – regular exercise is best not as an 'aside', but rather as a natural part of everyday life and is the best source of longevity;
- wake up each day with positive expectations, with things to achieve, with meaning and purpose to engage in activities we value, appreciate and feel good about;
- avoid stressful surroundings which are the source of angst, of noise, of hurry, of annoyance, of too much bustle and challenge, and have time for quietness, time to reflect, to relax, to play, to nap;
- eat well but eat less; reduce our calorie intake by 20 per cent, eat a good healthy breakfast, have an emphasis on vegetables, fruit and natural food and only small and infrequent amounts of meat; eat our meals with people we like, away from the distractions of TV, of 24-hour news channels, and be appreciative of the gifts we are sharing;
- enjoy some wine (moderate drinkers live longer than non-drinkers); enjoy a glass or two with our evening meal, when possible in the company of someone we prize;
- build a supportive family or social circle; enjoy the children, look after our parents, meet up with our friends, make regular social contacts, build warmth and positive circumstances and memories;

6 <http://www.bluezones.com/live-longer/>.

- engage with, enjoy and support the community, be part of making it live and gel, providing activities for young and old, caring for the vulnerable, achieving things together, creating a forward-looking, positive, active context in which to live and thrive;
- build great and lasting circles of friendships with positive, supportive people who bring fun and stimulus into each others' lives.

Improving the Well-being of a City

Dan Buettner[7] has taken the findings of his research into 'Blue Zones' and applied it to achieving significant change in urban areas. Supported by National Geographic magazine, in cooperation with Gallup's worldwide research and the World Database of Happiness, Dan identified the nine key factors of Blue Zones that make the difference. He calls these features 'Power 9' and you can hear him enthuse about his findings at:
www.ted.com/talks/dan_buettner_how_to_live_to_be_100.html

In 2009 Dan Buettner[8] and his 'Blue Zone' team led a project to promote the elements of 'Power 9' in an urban environment. His mission is to take 'the world's best practices in longevity and well-being to work in people's lives'. The people of the city of Albert Lea in Minnesota (a statistically average American city) were introduced to the principles that research had identified were central to 'Blue Zone' living[9].

---

7 <http://www.bluezones.com/about/dan-buettner/>.
8 Dan Buettner, Thrive: Finding Happiness the Blue Zones Way (National Geographic Society, 2010).
9 The excellent Blue Zones website will help you assess your own happiness levels and potential longevity if you Visit: <http://www.bluezones.com>.

Participants completed a one-year community health experiment, which followed Dan Buettner's Power 9 Principles under four categories:

- **Move Naturally** – just move, build activity into your everyday life, don't 'pump iron', join gyms, etc.
- **Right Outlook** – find positive purpose and reduce stress and pace of life.
- **Eat and Drink Wisely** – 20 per cent less to eat and a 'plant slant' - one to two drinks of wine a day with friends and/or family.
- **Connect** – belong to social groups, faith groups, community groups, have strong family links, committed relationships, invest in your children, be part of strong friendship circles, associate with positive people.

The results for the people of Albert Lea were remarkable. Life expectancy was raised by three years, the health care costs of city workers were reduced by some 40 per cent, and a collective 12,000 pounds were lost from waistlines. Dan's programme created a 'perfect storm' of health and happiness. He is now taking it to other American cities.

Health and Happiness at a National Level

'Too much and too long, we seem to have surrendered community excellence and community values in the mere accumulation of material things. The Gross National Product (GNP) includes air pollution and advertising for cigarettes, and ambulances to clear our highways of carnage. It counts special locks for our doors, and jails for the people who break them. GNP includes the destruction of the redwoods and the death of Lake Superior. It grows with the production of napalm and missiles and nuclear warheads. And if GNP includes all this, there is much that it does not comprehend. It does not focus on the health of our families, the quality of their education, or the joy of their play. It is indifferent to the decency of our factories and the safety of our streets alike. It does not include the beauty of our poetry or the strength of our marriages, or the intelligence of our public debate or the integrity of our public officials. GNP measures neither our wit nor our courage, neither our wisdom nor our learning, neither our compassion nor our devotion to our country. It [GNP] measures everything, in short, except that which makes life worthwhile.'

Robert F. Kennedy, 18 March 1968

Robert Kennedy's wisdom and foresight may have influenced others. In 1972 at the age of 17, Jigme Singye Wangchuck, after the sudden death of his father, was crowned King of the Himalayan nation of Bhutan.[10] He declared, most maturely and wisely, that during his reign he would be more concerned with Gross National Happiness (GNH) than with Gross Domestic Product (GDP) because the latter, in itself, does not necessarily lead to the well-being of a population. Taking longer to pick up the theme but getting there, governments of more developed countries, notably the UK, Germany and France, have in the last decade begun to think and speak in the same terms, committing to finding broader measures of the flourishing of their nation than simply economic productivity.

Through collaborating with an international group of scholars and researchers, the Centre for Bhutan Studies decided to focus on eight general contributors to happiness in the nation:

- physical, mental and spiritual health;
- time-balance;
- social and community vitality;
- cultural vitality;
- education;
- living standards;
- good governance; and
- ecological vitality.[11]

The GNH framework reflects its Buddhist origins, but is also based upon the research findings of Positive Psychology on happiness and well-being.

contributors to happiness

---

10 <http://www.time.com/time/health/article/0,8599,1016266,00.html#ixzz1Pj5NgRvR>.
11 <http://en.wikipedia.org/wiki/Gross_National_Happiness>.

home and happiness

The search in all this is for measures that say more about the happiness and contentment of a people, their satisfaction with their lives, the quality of relationships and community and family life, the standard of education and public health, the peacefulness and lawfulness of towns and cities, the protection of the environment, the flourishing of the arts, the level of satisfaction with working lives, the amount of purpose and meaning that people feel, the readiness to participate in democracy and public life, the experience of increasing standards of living, and generally the potential and capacity to live happier lives.

Happiest Places in the UK[12]

Researchers, using data from the British Household Panel Survey, drew up a 'happiness map' of England, Scotland and Wales based on people's assessment of their own level of well-being. This was the basis for a 'Top 10 list of the happiest places', which suggested that 8 out of the 10 are in Scotland or the north of England (the London Borough of Sutton was one of the few places in the south to do well).

The happiest places were reported as being:
- Powys in Wales (most sparsely populated county in Wales)
- Manchester
- West Lothian
- Cumbernauld, Kilsyth and Monklands
- Macclesfield.
-

...and the least happy as:
- Edinburgh
- Cynon Valley and Rhondda
- Amber Valley and North-east Derbyshire
- Clydesdale; Cumnock and the Don Valley; Kyle and Carrick
- Swansea.

least happy places

---

12 <http://news.bbc.co.uk/1/hi/health/7584321.stm> reporting the work of Dr Dimitris Ballas and Dr Mark Tranmer.

Some very interesting analysis accompanied the simple listings. This sought to identify the basis for people rating the area they lived in as happy or not. The researchers' observations suggested that:
- The ratings say more about people's personal circumstances than they do about geography or location (two former coal mining areas in Wales where the pits had been closed were less happy than the rest of the UK).
- The ratings are more to do with employment prospects, levels of health and supportive services, and educational opportunity and attainment than to do with geography.
- People who are unemployed are likely to be happier living somewhere where many others are without work, than they would be living somewhere where 'everyone has jobs'.
- People who have lived in an area for five years or longer are likely to be happier than less settled people.
- People living in areas where there are strong interpersonal relationships and good social contacts will be happier than those who live in less close communities.
- People who live in areas where there is less inequality in living standards will be happier than those living where there are wide wealth differentials.

The researchers were keen to point out that their work was not claiming that 'geographical location was a significant factor in determining happiness' though Dr. Ballas did add 'There really is something about the intrinsic nature of places which can influence happiness and well-being. The environment, lack of green spaces, air and noise pollution and crime rates all influence happiness.'

Best Cities to Live in

Research projects[13] do distinguish between 'happiest populations' and 'best cities to live in'. A recent survey suggested that the best world city to live in was Vienna because 'The Austrian capital, with its ornate buildings,

home and happiness

public parks and extensive bicycle network recently reduced the cost of its annual public transport ticket to 1 euro a day. Serious crime is rare and the city of around 1.7 million inhabitants regularly tops global quality of life surveys.'

The top five cities were:
1. Vienna, Austria
2. Zurich, Switzerland
3. Auckland, New Zealand
4. Munich, Germany
5. Dusseldorf, Germany.

The report does go on to warn European cities that their dominance may not last if the current financial crisis reduces living standards across the continent.

In last place in the survey was Baghdad, for fairly obvious reasons, and the cities in the Arab countries of North Africa and the Middle East were all recognised as suffering currently from the struggle by their citizens for democracy and greater freedom.

---

13 <http://news.yahoo.com/vienna-best-place-live-baghdad-worst-survey-121226526.html>.

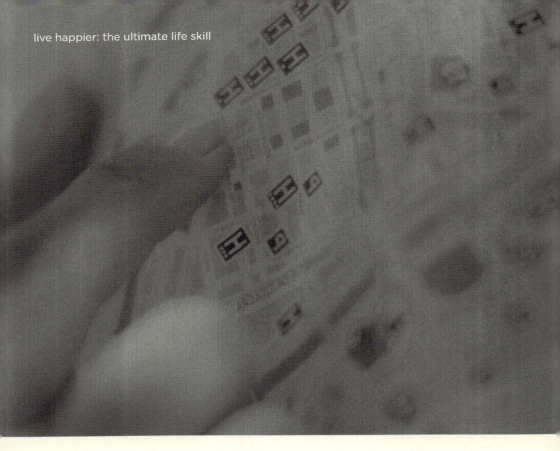

Where Does all this Leave Us?

For most of us the place we live will not have been arrived at after great analysis and choice from many options. Many of us will live close to where we were born and grew up, or in a place that our education or work has taken us, or somewhere we moved to as a result of a relationship or having a family. It's likely that our home will have been chosen based on income and space needs, and in an area that provides good access to work, education and health needs. It is extremely unlikely we will have found a haven after working through a checklist of Power 9 possibilities; life is never that perfect. So, how would you assess the place you live and its contribution to your happiness level?

Life Skill: Create a Live Happier Environment

Activity 1: 'Now'

Reflect on the material provided in this chapter and decide how important the place where you currently live is to your happiness.

Mark with a X

Very important

Fairly important

Not important

What are the factors that make you decide that?

_____

_____

_____

Activity 2: 'Next'

Here are some of the factors that make for healthier, happier living in the 'Blue Zones'. Work out whether any of those factors are available in the place you live now.

Answer 'Yes' if that factor exists for you or 'No' if it doesn't.

The activity assumes you are basically healthy. If you have any health conditions that limit your capacity for exercise then you may need to pass on the first section or answer in the light of your level of mobility.

Good for Exercise
Live happier places have exercise 'built into them' or make exercise easy to access. Do you have:

Stairs to climb	Yes	No
Shops to walk to	Yes	No
Parks to walk in	Yes	No
Friends in the area you visit	Yes	No
Family members you visit	Yes	No
Places of entertainment within walking distance	Yes	No
Religious centres you walk to	Yes	No
Cafes, restaurants, local pubs	Yes	No

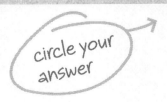

circle your answer

home and happiness

Children's playgrounds	Yes	No
Community centres you visit	Yes	No
Libraries or galleries you use	Yes	No
Sports centres you use	Yes	No
Other features that cause you to exercise	Yes	No

Total   **'Yes's**

Good Social Contacts

Live happier places allow lots of social contacts. Do you have:

Regular visitors to your home	Yes	No
Friends/neighbours/family you visit	Yes	No
Neighbourhood groups you are part of	Yes	No
Religious groups you are part of	Yes	No
Sports teams you play in	Yes	No
A book club you are part of	Yes	No
Coffee mornings, wine clubs, etc.	Yes	No
'Nights out' with friends	Yes	No
Adult education classes	Yes	No

Film clubs you are part of	Yes	No
Sports team training sessions	Yes	No
A walking group	Yes	No
Resident/neighbourhood groups	Yes	No
Works outings	Yes	No
Friends you eat out with	Yes	No
Other ways of meeting people	Yes	No
Total	**'Yes's**	

home and happiness

A Positive Environment
Live happier environments offer us positive prospects. Do you live in an area which offers:

Good employment opportunities	Yes	No
Good education prospects	Yes	No
An active purposeful community	Yes	No
A community with few inequalities	Yes	No
Good health care facilities	Yes	No
Good, all round support services	Yes	No
Regular cultural events	Yes	No
Security and little crime	Yes	No
Parks and green spaces	Yes	No
Little air or noise pollution	Yes	No
Acceptable traffic levels	Yes	No
Good public transport facilities	Yes	No
Easy access to theatres/concert halls	Yes	No
Easy access to stations/airports/public transport	Yes	No

circle your answer

Easy access to beach or countryside

Other positive environmental features

Total   'Yes's

A Positive Home Environment

Live happier lives can be influenced by a positive home environment. Does your home offer you:

An attractive living space	Yes	No
Warm and bright living conditions	Yes	No
Bright décor which cheers the spirit	Yes	No
Good lighting which helps you work and relax	Yes	No
Plants and/or flowers	Yes	No
Access to music when you like it	Yes	No
A comfortable eating area	Yes	No
Photos that cheer you	Yes	No
Examples of art and craft you enjoy	Yes	No
Books and papers you enjoy	Yes	No

circle your answer

home and happiness

A sleeping area that comforts and relaxes you	Yes	No
A garden or outside area	Yes	No
Room to welcome friends o	Yes	No
Space for pets if they make you happy	Yes	No
Other features that please you	Yes	No
Total	'Yes's	
Grand Total (a possible 60 'Yes's)	'Yes's	

How did you do?

Over 40 'Yes's probably means you are generally happy with where you live but it is worth pondering the 'No's to see whether there are any changes you can make to increase that score.

20 to 39 'Yes's means you are halfway there and could consider how you might become more alert to things you might change in the future.

Less than 20 'Yes's gives you plenty of scope to seek opportunities in the future to find or create environments that support you in living happier.

On the basis of your reflections on your current home and happiness, and the information you have worked with in this section write in what you would like more of, less of and what you would like to keep the same in your life right now. Reflect on your home and your environment and plan any changes you would like to make.

More of	Less of	Keep the same

Choose three that you would like to start working on right now.

1.
2.
3.

home and happiness

"The supreme happiness in life is the conviction that we are loved – loved for ourselves, or rather, loved in spite of ourselves."
Victor Hugo, Writer and Political Activist

spirituality

we should all learn this

'The world has to learn that the actual pleasure derived from material things is of a rather low quality on the whole and less even in quantity than it looks to those who have not tried it.'
Oliver Wendell Holmes, Poet

 livehappier.com

Spirituality and Happiness

What is Known About Spirituality and Happiness?

It is important to distinguish here between spirituality and religion. The Oxford Dictionary of English defines 'religion' as:

'The belief in and worship of a superhuman controlling power, especially a personal god or gods; a particular system of faith and worship.'

And 'spirituality' as:

'Relating to or affecting the human spirit or soul as opposed to material or physical things; having a relationship based on a profound level of mental or emotional communion.'

A Eurobarometer poll in 2005 reported that 38 percent 'believed there is a God',
40 percent believe there is 'some sort of spirit or life force' and 20 percent answered 'I don't believe there is any sort of spirit, God or life force'.[1]

Religion has been seen by some as causing conflicts and dividing the world and its peoples, in an age where we are becoming more conscious of living in one 'global village'.

---

1 'Eurobarometer: Social Values, Science and Technology', European Commission, June 2005.

Spirituality and Religion - Clearly not the Same[2]

In some parts of the West, organised religion has been losing its attraction and many of its followers. At the same time, there has been increased interest in 'spirituality'.

Dissatisfaction with dogma, with creeds, with claims to be 'God's chosen people', with the condemnation and rejection of rival faiths, with clerical domination and abuse, with sexist structures and attachment to outdated moral strictures, has resulted in many leaving the churches but developing a need to search for a spiritual dimension to their lives.

The traditional religions of the West have seen significant declines in church attendance, but that turning away does not always bring the answers to many of the 'big questions'. Many are searching instead in other directions for 'spiritual meaning' in their lives.

The Positive Psychology Focus

Positive Psychology research[3] has been very interested in exploring the relationship between religion, spirituality, well-being and happiness. The research indicates that religious people in most countries appear to be slightly but significantly happier (and healthier) than people of no religion. This is true only if the religions are 'prosocial'[4] (i.e., if they avoid preaching about a hateful, vengeful God and a worthless, contemptible, lost humanity).

What interested the researchers most were the components of *religious* participation that brought positive benefits.

---

2   Diarmuid O'Murchu, Religion In Exile: A Spiritual Vision for the Homeward Bound (Gateway, 2000).
3   See research on spirituality, religion and happiness reported in: Ed Diener and Robert Biswas-Diener, Happiness: unlocking the Mysteries of Psychological Wealth (Blackwell, 2008); Martin E.P. Seligman, Authentic Happiness (Nicholas Brealey Publishing, 2003); Alan Carr, Positive Psychology: the science of happiness and human strengths (Routledge, 2004).
4   Wikipedia: 'Prosocial behavior is caring about the welfare and rights of others, feeling concern and empathy

These appear to be:
- having a faith that consoles and comforts, that promises positive outcomes in troubled times, that makes some sense of an imperfect world and can even 'take the sting' out of one of life's biggest negatives, death itself;
- having an early grounding in community, in family, in moral living that shapes character and teaches love, compassion, awe, transcendence and the avoidance of selfishness (these benefits continue even if religious practice falls away);
- the social support that comes from being part of a diverse community with shared values and beliefs, and the experience and solidarity of collective worship;
- the positive emotions that can be triggered by magnificent churches, colourful, moving ceremonies and beautiful religious art, prayer and music;
- participation in something old, with a long historical significance and continuing importance;
- a source of finding 'meaning' in life, to engagement with causes, to ideals that enable us to contribute to something that 'is bigger than ourselves', all key components of living happier.

The 'Big' Questions

Many who reject organised religion still experience a need to answer for themselves 'the big questions' of life:

- 'What is life all about, what is its purpose?'
- 'Why are we here?'
- 'Are we meant to be happy and, if so, how do we do it?'
- 'What is success in life and how will I achieve it?'
- 'What do I believe about relationships, about fidelity, about family, about community and society, and about wealth?'
- 'What are my ambitions and goals in life?'
- 'What do I want my reputation to be, what do I want my legacy to be?'

ask yourself

Some 'Answers'?

For somebody who has a strictly material and scientific view of human beings and the world, then the answers may be uncomplicated. Maybe we really are just a mass of DNA, with a limited lifespan, with a capacity to breed and perpetuate our species, to do what the genes require and what our appetites and needs demand, for as long as we can keep going, and then die as peacefully and painlessly as possible.

For other people, that strictly physical view of the human does not feel or sound quite right and is not totally aligned with their experience of life. In being born, in loving others, in experiencing the highs and lows of life, in friendships, in teams, in achievements, in giving birth, in losing and burying, in the wonders, beauty and power of nature, in the rhythms of the seasons, in the vastness of the universe, in many contexts we sense a dimension beyond the merely physical.

spirituality and happiness

'The spiritual quest begins, for most people, as a search for meaning.'
Marilyn Ferguson, Humanistic Psychologist

What is Spiritual?

Spirituality is interpreted in different ways, as having to do with:
- a non-material, non-physical part of ourselves or our world;
- that which is at the heart of us, the very essence of us;
- 'our very soul and spirit' that makes us who we are;
- connecting with and experiencing 'the beyond' in our lives;
- a focus on creation, or nature, or a sense of order in the universe;
- finding answers to the big questions of life;
- addressing our 'smallness against the vastness of the universe', giving us opinions on ourselves and others, on the world, on existence;
- an emotional response to major life events such as birth, death, love, loss;
- reflecting on life events and experiences that bring feelings of significance, unity, acceptance, connection, serenity, joy, reconciliation, celebration, transcendence, happiness.

'Happiness comes from spiritual wealth, not material wealth. Happiness comes from giving, not getting. If we bring happiness to others, we cannot stop it coming to us also. To get joy, we must give it and keep it and to keep joy, we must scatter it.' John Templeton, Businessman and Philanthropist

Finding Spirituality

'We are not human beings having a spiritual experience. We are spiritual beings having a human experience.'
Pierre Teilhard de Chardin, Philosopher

- Spiritual stimulus can come from religion, meditation, music, literature, poetry, friendship, conviviality.
- A sense of spirituality can be experienced in the comradeship of people who share extreme challenges or adversity together.
- It can be triggered by awesome natural settings (landscapes and seascapes) or events, by night skies, dawns, changing seasons, sunsets, or vast silences.
- It has been encouraged by rituals and ceremonies, by the celebration of a New Year, by shared community experiences.
- Some have found it in sporting or other bonding experiences (e.g. demonstrations in support of causes such as civil rights, peace protests, etc.).
- Some have sensed a spiritual dimension in liberating political movements, for example in the outlawing of slavery, in the Feminist Movement, in the Black Consciousness Movement against apartheid in South Africa, in the resistance by monks, students and the oppressed to the brutal regime in Burma, inspired by Aung San Suu Kyi.
- Gandhi himself used the spiritual dimension of his Indian culture to inspire his campaign of non-violent resistance to British rule.
- Nelson Mandela's philosophy of non-reprisal against the oppressive white regime, after 25 years behind bars, spoke volumes to many of a spiritual vision for his country's future, as did 'the dream' of Martin Luther King of a future of freedom and equality for Black Americans.

And Some Would Say:
- Our unique, individual 'stories' (our life histories) have a spiritual element. Sharing them with others, and recognising and respecting achievements and uniqueness, can build relationships with a spiritual dimension.
- We grow and prosper only through loving and being loved; such experiences give us an inkling of a bigger potential experience.
- The public expression of love after disasters such as 9/11, or the tsunamis, are examples of love made visible on a vast scale.
- Spirituality is apparent in statements such as those in the 'Universal Declaration of Human Rights', in the Geneva Convention, in the opening statements of the American Constitution.

'The spiritual journey is individual, highly personal. It cannot be organised or regulated. It isn't true that everybody should follow one path. Listen to your own truth.'
Ram Dass, Spiritual Teacher

Spirituality in this sense addresses our personal integrity, our relationships with others, the values that underpin how we live our lives.

While religions can address the hope of an afterlife, spirituality can focus on:
- the 'horizontal, the here and now, on transcendence';
- an engagement with 'otherness';
- our fellow human beings;
- our world, its wonder and potential; and
- the world's well-being.

Spirituality can detect a sense of purpose, order and wholeness in the universe. This kind of spirituality takes a long view and finds more than the ordinariness of everyday life. This is a spirituality which is addressing 'why are we here?' It motivates us to work for what we care deeply about. Connecting values and purpose can be a spiritual force.

'There is no higher religion than human service. To work for the common good is the gentlest creed.' Albert Einstein, Physicist

Spirituality motivates us to work for interdependence, for connectedness, for universalism, for sustainability, for the removal of divisions, for the good of humanity and 'creation'.

Spirituality Elsewhere

Some architects recognise a spiritual dimension in buildings – they work to design places, which 'inspire', encourage and motivate those who will live and work in them.

'When the spirit does not work with the hand there is no art.'
Leonardo Da Vinci, Italian Renaissance Polymath

There is a growing interest in the links between spirituality and the workplace.
'Each of us will spend more of our waking hours working, or preparing for work, or recovering from work, than we spend on any other activity in our whole life ... At the end of each day the universe is different (from what) it was at the beginning, and our work is one of the most important aspects of that change.'[5]

---

5 Liz Hollis, 'It's work but not as we know it', The Guardian, 15 September 2007.

spirituality and happiness

In 'It's work but not as we know it', a 2007 article by Liz Hollis[6] exploring what the workplace will look like in 2017, futurist Anne Lise Kjaer predicts that the workplace will have to change radically between 2007 and 2017 to attract the new generation of 'e-lancers'.

She predicts that there will need to be: a 'home-from-home vibe', with giant communal desks, showers, 'chill-out' zones, and a 'pod' for power naps after virtual meetings across time zones, to attract e-lancers in two days a week at times of their choice.

Kjaer predicts, 'Within a few years, the very phrase "going to work" will be meaningless. Work will be what we do, not a place we go to.'

She believes these trends will drive the changes:
- smart technology;
- globalisation;
- the rise of the Asian economies;
- increased female empowerment;
- increasing spiritual and emotional awareness.

She observes we are entering 'an emotional decade' in which 'ethics and spirituality will prevail in the workplace'. People are discovering that money alone doesn't buy happiness and they will be looking elsewhere for 'meaning'. To attract and retain the people they need, businesses will have to go beyond the salary package.

---

6 Richard A. Bowell, The 7 Steps of Spiritual Intelligence – the Practical Pursuit of Purpose, Success and Happiness (Nicholas Brealey Publishing, London, 2004).

They will need to 'empower workers and enhance their physical and mental well-being too. We will want work to be life-enhancing and the companies we work for to be ethical. We will be looking for emotional connection and empowerment on all levels.'

With people investing so much time in work, then the challenge must be to make it meaningful and motivating. Individuals and teams working for higher goals, seeking achievements that benefit others beyond themselves, are likely to achieve levels of commitment and self-actualisation that bring success and reputation to their organisation.

'Human systems are also patterns of dynamic energy...From this perspective it's no longer about "me and you" but about "us". It's not separation; it's integration. It's not isolation; it's an understanding that we are all part of one great big interwoven system. These new ideas are critical to understanding how we can make shifts in organisational culture, collaboration and teamwork.'[7]

Danah Zohar discussing her book 'SQ, Connecting with Our Spiritual Intelligence'

Some psychologists and brain experts now recognise that rather than just the traditional view that we each have an IQ, we do, in fact, have many types of intelligence, including Emotional Intelligence and Spiritual Intelligence.

---

7 <http://dzohar.com/www2/?page_id=8>.

Where Next?

Links are also being explored between physical and mental health and religion and spirituality. The suggestion is that a strong religious or spiritual life can assist in helping us cope with:
- ageing;
- physical and mental illness;
- crises and bereavements.

This is achieved by increasing our involvement in healthy living, in increasing our social support and injecting meaning into our lives.

Other Aspects of Spirituality

Research by HSBC[8] established that different countries have different attitudes to old age and retirement. The British see it as a time for self-sufficiency, independence, flexibility and personal responsibility. Americans see it as a time for opportunity, new careers and spiritual fulfilment.

In March 2007, Canadian Philosopher Charles Taylor, aged 75, won the £800,000 Templeton Prize for Progress Toward Research or Discoveries about Spiritual Realities. His work linked a search for meaning to the recruitment of young people to terrorist groups. He warns: 'There are certain kinds of hunger that people have, including a sense of meaning in life, that comprises the spiritual dimension. ... These terrorists are motivated by the need to be connected to a big cause. The only way they can be prevented from heading for terrorism is to have a better answer to the meaningfulness of life.'

'He who has a "why" to live for can bear almost any "how".'
Nietzsche, Philosopher

---

8 <http://www.hsbc.com/1/PA_esf-ca-app-content/content/assets/retirement/2005_for_report.pdf>.

Activity 1: How Spiritual Are You?

Reflect on the statements below and how much they apply to you. Score them as follows:

0 = Does not apply **1 = Somewhat applies** **2 = Very much applies**

Spirituality in Life Generally

1. I have a sense that there is more to life than the physical, material world that we experience every day.

2. I believe that my life has meaning, purpose and value beyond material gain or reward.

3. People looking at the way I work and my lifestyle would guess I am motivated by things other than 'the material' things in life.

4. I can describe myself without referring to my job and have pride in that description.

write your scores

5. It is very important to me to have a reputation for:

- Honesty
- Truth
- Compassion
- Generosity
- Peacemaking
- Patience
- Integrity
- Cooperation

- Gratitude
- Loyalty
- Love
- Friendship
- Teamwork
- Empathy
- Creating unity

6. I work hard to build such a reputation.

7. I frequently reflect on life and my part in it and wonder what I can do to make things better.

8. I give time regularly to reflect and ponder on 'the bigger questions'; reflecting on my purpose, meaning and contribution in life.

score 0 to 2 here

9. People report having experienced spiritual moments in particular settings such as: at the birth of their child; at a great musical performance; in the presence of great works of art; in beautiful natural settings, landscapes, seascapes; in gardening and working with nature; in witnessing the force of nature in storms or earthquakes; in moments of great threat or fear or near-death situations; at a moment of outstanding achievement; in a loving relationship; at the loss of a loved one; etc.

    I know what they mean because I have had a similar experience.

10. I have found a spiritual dimension in my religious beliefs.

11. I believe a spiritual dimension in life helps me to live happier.

score 0 to 2 here

spirituality and happiness

Spirituality at Work

12. I believe people are much more than their work, their salary level and the status of their job.

13. I believe I am more than my work, my salary level and the status of my job.

14. I commit to high performance, believing we should each offer the best of our talents and gifts to the 'common good'.

15. I genuinely rejoice in the achievements of others.

16. I prize highly being a member of a team and sharing in collective performance.

17. I make great effort in building positive relationships with colleagues, customers and even competitors.

score 0 to 2 here

18. I make great efforts to make the workplace a happy and positive place.

19. I am appreciative of the support and encouragement I get from others.

20. I experience pride in creating products, services or results that benefit society.

21. I enjoy working in a culture in which respect and compassion for people is apparent.

22. I believe that people are the most important resource in an organisation.

23. I am committed to my continuing development, as I want to make the most of all my potential.

24. I can see a spiritual dimension to the work I do.

Spirituality in the Community and the World

25. I give time and effort in contributing to the betterment of my local community.

spirituality and happiness

26. I give my time and abilities to working for the disadvantaged. I am committed to and spend time on causes that benefit others without material return for me.

27. I am conscious of the challenges in conserving the planet and make strong efforts to avoid excess and reduce waste.

28. I contribute to groups and causes that work for peace in the world, for the reduction of poverty and hunger in the developing world, and for the promotion of a 'one world' future.

'Ethical existence is the highest manifestation of spirituality.'
Albert Schweitzer, Theologian

'Life becomes harder for us when we live for others ... but it also becomes richer and happier.'
Albert Schweitzer, Theologian

Spiritual Growth

I participate in activities that enhance my spiritual development such as:

29. Meditation on the 'big questions'. Listening to inspiring and moving music.

30. Reading spiritually inspiring literature.

31. Working to create positives out of negatives.

32. Forgiving and asking for forgiveness.

33. Problem-solving and peacemaking.

34. Activities that 'give back' to individuals and communities some of the things I have been lucky enough to receive.

Total your score and reflect on what that score might suggest to you.

The total possible is 100.

wirte your total here

spirituality and happiness

Scoring 0 to 20
It seems that spirituality plays little part in your life at the moment. You seem to have no need of it or interest in it and can live your life happily without that dimension.

Scoring 21 to 60
You are engaged with spirituality and given the opportunity and motivation you might take your interests further. You might expand your exploration into areas or sources beyond those you currently relate to and benefit from doing so.

Score 61 to 100
You seem to have experience of and interest in spirituality and it may already play a significant part in your life. You possibly accept the spiritual view that development is limitless and will continue to advance your engagement with and pursuit of higher levels of spiritual awareness and application. Enjoy the journey!

'Some day, after we have mastered the winds, the waves, the tides and gravity we shall harness the energies of love. Then, for the second time in the history of the world, humankind will have discovered fire.'
Pierre Teilhard de Chardin, Philosopher

Activity 2: My Legacy

Planning and working to make our lives happier and helping others to do the same will be time well spent. There are no guarantees it will work out entirely, but it will certainly give others and us more chance of fulfilment. There is, of course, one thing that is true for all of us in life: 'no one gets out of here alive'.

Hopefully our lives will be stories of great relationships, memorable achievements and significant happiness but, without being morbid, we are not going to last forever. It can help us order our future to reflect on what we would like our legacy to be when our time is up. What will we hope those who survive us will remember about us? What will they say about us, about our qualities or otherwise, about our 'contribution'?

In some sense this is a 'spiritual' question. We will not be 'around' in a physical sense, but we will have a presence at least in the minds and memories of many people: our partners, our children and grandchildren if we had them, our brothers, sisters, cousins, colleagues and certainly our friends.

Imagine being able to sit in on a conversation about you in a group gathered to remember you.

Who could be there? (think family, friends, colleagues, etc.)

spirituality and happiness

What would they say about:

Your character and personality?
_____
_____

Your qualities, strengths and weaknesses?
_____
_____

The difference you made to their lives?
_____
_____
_____

Your contribution to 'family'?
_____
_____
_____

Your contribution to friendships?

Your contribution to work life?

Your contribution to teams you were part of?

Your contribution to the wider community?

Your contribution to the wider world?

Your contribution to good causes?

write your thoughts here

spirituality and happiness

Your contribution to the development of others?

What they will miss most about you?

What you will be best rememberd for?

Your key achievements?

Are you living now with the priorities that will mean you are best remembered for the things you want to be remembered for? Do you need to change anything to make your legacy more like you would like it to be?

What are your reflections on this chapter?

spirituality and happiness

Finding Out More...

- Do an internet search for: 'spiritual intelligence'; 'types of intelligence'; 'Maslow and spirituality'; 'spirituality and health'; 'religion and health'; 'happiness'; 'science of happiness'; 'politics and happiness'; 'happiness research.
- Look at the following websites:
  - www.spiritualprogressives.org
  - www.yoursoulatwork.com

Some more reading:
- Tony Buzan, The power of spiritual intelligence (Thorsens, London, 2001).
- Bryan A. Hiebert, Your soul at work: how to live your values in the workplace (Northstone Publishing Inc., 2005).
- Nicholas Weiller, Your soul at work (Cowley Publications, USA, 2003).
- Diarmuid O'Murchu, Religion in exile: a spiritual homecoming (Crossroad Publishing, 2000).

On the basis of your reflections in this section write in what you would like more of, less of and what you would like to keep the same in the next phase of your life.

More of	Less of	Keep the same

spirituality and happiness

Choose three that you would like to start exploring now:
1.
2.
3.

'Spirituality is being concerned with things of the spirit – the big questions of meaning, metaphysics, existence. Being spiritual is thinking about, wondering about and exploring the deepest aspects of reality, values, morals and meanings.' Amara Rose, www.helpguide.org

Other Life Skills Programmes connected with Spirituality and Happiness that you may want to consider as they appear on www.livehappier.com **are:**
- **Be Grateful**
- **Live the Good Life**
- **Find Meaning**
- **Mindful and Meditative**
- **Make Others Happy**

live happier: the ultimate life skill

It's time now to review your work, to revisit the 'More of, Less of' matrices at the end of each chapter and ask yourself:

it's time to review your work

what next?

livehappier.com

Where do you go from here?

As you have worked through the different chapters of this book you will have accumulated lots of information about your thoughts on your life and your happiness. You will have pondered some changes you might like to make, and the goals and ambitions you want to pursue in the quest to live happier and help others do the same.

It's time now to review your work, to revisit the 'More of Less of' matrices at the end of each chapter and ask yourself:
- What am **I** going to do to live happier?
- What am I going to do to help **others** to live happier?

As we say at the start of the book, change comes from awareness and ACTION.

As you review the work you have done, reflect further and ask yourself:
- What is the picture I have built up about my life so far - the skills, strengths, knowledge and experiences I have to carry me into the next phase of my life?
- What are the hopes and ambitions I have for 'living happier'?
- What balance am I looking for in the different arenas of my life?
- What are the challenges that lie ahead?
- What do I feel most motivated to change at this stage?
-

You need now to pull together the full picture and identify what you want to make happen in the next phase of your life.

Activity 1: My Live Happier Mind Map

Many have found that a 'Mind Map' can provide a helpful framework for planning. It is a very useful technique, invented by Tony Buzan[1], for working with lots of information and making it manageable. It can help as a way of generating and recording data and making it usable and it beats making lots of lists.

Lists are linear and difficult to interconnect. A Mind Map is more in tune with the way our brains work, i.e. not in straight lines but spontaneous, multidimensional and interconnecting.

On the following page is a Mind Map compiled by someone planning ahead after using the Live Happier material in this book and facing a range of key questions and opportunities.

You can see that the Mind Map method:
- Can contain masses of diverse but interconnected ideas with the main themes clearly defined.
- Can ease the task of selecting priorities and areas to work on while seeing the 'big picture'.
- Offers more coherence whilst being easy to add to or expand.

If you are contemplating or facing adjustments in your life after working through this book, building your own Mind Map could alert you to some of the areas you will be keen to address. Here's how...

---

1 See <http://www.imindmap.com>.

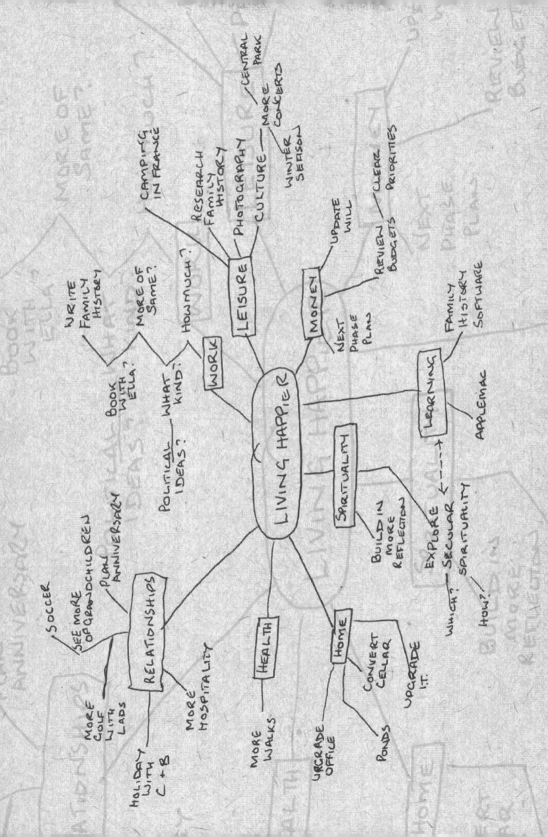

Mind Map Method

Working on a large sheet of paper put the title of your Mind Map right at the centre – Living Happier.

To that centre add the heading for the first of the themes you will think through – think in terms of branch lines leaving the main line stations and heading outwards to suburbs. Start anywhere with any topic.

Write the theme headings in capitals or in different colours.

Reflecting on the relevant areas of your life and your happiness, *let your mind flow around each theme and develop your lines of thought leading outwards*. As thoughts come to mind enter the key words that occur to you on the line.

Think through and build your Mind Map around the different areas of your life that you will wish to address as you seek to live happier. Take your time, it's valuable work!

Analysing Your Mind Map

When you have completed your Mind Map, study it carefully and, as you do, enter your answers to the following questions:

- Where are the 'satisfiers' in my life – the things that bring me most satisfaction and happiness? (Mark these with a √)
- Where are the dissatisfactions for me – the things I would like less of or would like to change? (Mark these with a X)
- Are there things that link up and can be addressed together? (Draw in any links using dotted lines.)
- Look again. Is there anything missing that should be on there? If so, add it now.

ask yourself

What next?

What are the most important messages for me from this live happier 'picture' as I contemplate the next phase of my life?

_____

_____

_____

What are the things I most want to do something about?

_____

_____

_____

Are there any surprises for me on my Mind Map? If so, what are they?

_____

_____

_____

Which areas of my life require my attention and action as a priority?

What differences am I looking for in each of the arenas of my life that I have worked on?

Who are the key people in my life?

write your thoughts here

What next?

What will I do to maintain and enhance those relationships?

Where do I get the support that I might need to make the changes I want and how might I make best use of that?

Now summarise what you want in the matrix below.

On the basis of your reflections write in on this matrix YOUR PRIORITIES.

What would you like more of, less of and what you would like to keep the same in your life right now?

	More of	Less of	Keep the same
My Relationships			
My Work			
My Money			
My Health			
My Leisure			

What next?

My Learning			
My Home			
My Spirituality			

Life Skill: Set Clear Objectives

If you don't know where you are going you could finish up somewhere else!

What are the three most important things you want to work on?

1. _____

2. _____

3. _____

Take each of these in turn and work through the following steps to identify clear objectives that will help you achieve what you are seeking.

What next?

State each objective clearly by starting with the word

'To ....' and following this with an action word (e.g. 'To take a course in web design to further my skills and increase my chance of promotion.' Or 'To have more quality time with my youngest daughter.')

Objectives

1. To

2. To

3. To

4. To

5. To

6. To

Check that your objective passes the SMART test. Is it:
- **S**pecific – absolutely clearly stated?
- **M**easurable – will you know clearly when you have achieved it?
- **A**chievable – 'do-able'?
- **R**ealistic – do you truly believe you can do it and are you motivated to do so?
- **T**imely – does it have a clearly stated time frame (e.g. within 30 days) and do you have the time to commit to its achievement?

Work on each of your three priority objectives. Get them through the SMART test.

Activity 2: Action Planning

'We fail to achieve things we want for two reasons. Either our action plan is not good enough or we are not sufficiently motivated!'
Anon

An OBJECTIVE is something we WANT and AIM to achieve.
An ACTION PLAN is what we will DO and WHEN to achieve it.

'The constitution only gives people the right to pursue happiness. You have to catch it yourself!'
Benjamin Franklin, U.S. Statesman

	me	you	us	another group	the organisation	the system	society
now							
tomorrow							
soon							
sometime							the swamp
eventually							
never							

firm ground

The swamp picture warns us of the dangers of making loose, woolly, vague or remote action plans. The further we get from doing things OURSELVES and TODAY the more likely our plans will sink in the swamp!

Identify the objective you want to work on first.

Write down what YOU are going to DO about it and WHEN.

Stay out of the swamp!

Build up the action steps you will need to take in sequence to achieve the objective.

Action Plan 1

1. _____
2. _____
3. _____
4. _____

Action Plan 2

1. _____
2. _____
3. _____
4. _____

Action Plan 3

1. _____

2. _____

3. _____

4. _____

Decide when you will review progress and readjust action plans as necessary.

Work on your action plans for each objective. Decide priorities and action sequences and put your initial action steps into your diary.

If at first you don't succeed...

.... we live in a complex world and are involved and interact with other unique individuals. Not everything you set your heart on may be achieved and it will be important if that happens to draw back for a while and think again. Some would say that it is always sensible to have a Plan B, even as you are working on Plan A.

But, what if you come up against a situation you wish to be different and find that your efforts don't get you the results that you want? In that situation it is important to recognise you have some options.

You can

- **Try again to change things** – revise your action plan, recommit and who knows what difference persistence might make?
- **Leave it** – if something is very much not to your liking, if you have tried everything to change it without success, you can move out,

move away, move on. Fresh starts, if chosen, well-judged and prepared for can be fruitful.
- **Change ourselves** – if leaving is not possible or not to your liking then you can change yourself to make things better. You can change how you see things, change your ideas, change your focus, change your priorities, change how you deal with things. Changing yourself can change other people and change how you experience situations.
- **Live with it** – this means more than just shrugging your shoulders and surrendering. You can live more successfully with a situation you wish were different by focusing less on it and more on something else, by reducing the 'space' you give it in your thoughts or in your day. You can find attractive distractions that take your mind off the problem and reduce its significance, you can use your support system to 'get stuff off your chest', to 'share the problem', to 'give yourself a break', to learn to laugh at yourself or the world. Security means always having an alternative!

Activity 3: Putting Others in the Picture

While you have been focusing on your future, others have been attending to their present. They may be curious as to what you have been doing and what you may have in mind. You owe it to people who are special or important to you to share your thoughts and the possible implications.

Who do you need to speak to about your quest to live happier and the plans you are forming?

How are they likely to be affected by and react to what you hope to do?

What are the outcomes you are seeking?

What will be the best way to put them in the picture? When, where, how?

Activity 4: A Letter to Yourself

A very effective technique at this stage is to write an email to yourself that you can receive as a reminder in six months' time. You can do this if you visit: http://www.emailfuture.com
and you can choose any date in the future that you wish.

If you prefer the old technology, we invite you to write a letter to yourself and file it away to be opened in six months' time. Enter in your diary a reminder to retrieve that letter (remember to note where it is filed!)

Your letter should spell out clearly what you hope to have achieved for each of your priority objectives in the next six months.

Almost certainly, when the time comes you will have forgotten all about it, but it can be fun and useful to get a reminder of our intentions and ambitions and see how we have progressed our plans or how we may need to reassess them.

We truly hope that by this stage you will have demonstrated to yourself that you really can create your own future. By combining awareness and skills you really can make your life more like you want it to be.

Remember, luck is the crossroad where preparation and opportunity meet. Our objective has been to help you reach that crossroad and for you to visualise, plan and act to set off in the direction that is right for you and for those closest to you. So, you have given time and attention to your life review. Hopefully you have emerged with a clearer sense of direction and purpose, a motivation to live happier, and to make the changes you believe will help you achieve that.

The most important messages about the process and the live happier website are that you:

- make them your servant and not your master. Do not let anything you have read or done dictate to you;
- take charge of the material you have produced, own it, set objectives for what you want to be different, commit to the actions you decide to take;
- are clear that the most important elements in the process are you and those you care about; be sensitive as well as motivated;
- are prepared to adapt and reshape your plans, not everything will work out exactly as you wish;
- get plenty of support and encouragement and give that back to those who need it from you.

This is your life, it is yours to shape and be in charge of!

You really can be the architect of your future and find routes to happier lives for yourself and for others.

Barrie Hopson and Mike Scally

Acknowledgements

This book and website owe much to, and have been inspired by, the work of many who describe their professional discipline as 'Positive Psychology'.

We are particularly indebted to the work of Michael Argyle, Albert Bandura, Roy Baumeister, Tal Ben-Shahar, Robert Biswas-Diener, Nathaniel Branden, Mihaly Csikszentmihalyi, Edward Deci, Ed Diener, Albert Ellis, Robert Emmons, Barbara Fredrickson, Dan Gilbert, John Gottman, Daniel Kahneman, Ellen Langer, David Lykken, Sonya Lyubomirsky, Abraham Maslow, Ann Masten, Michael McCullough, #David Myers, Christopher Peterson, Tom Rath, Carl Rogers, Julian Rotter, Richard Ryan, Karen Reivich, Martin Seligman and Al Siebert. We have found the academic collection of the sources of the science of happiness by Alan Carr especially useful.

We are very committed to giving recognition to all our sources for any inclusions in our work and list these references in our footnotes. We will appreciate being made aware of any instance of a failure to do this and will ensure a prompt correction in any such case.

In the design of the ebook and the technology of the site we are especially appreciative of the work of a very talented group of individuals, who all share our vision of a happier world.

We are exceedingly grateful to our colleagues and fellow Directors: Danyl Bosomworth, Chris Soames, and Stuart Miller for the design and build of the website, for their most positive approach to every challenge and their commitment to the cause we all share.

We are additionally very thankful for the editing skills and support provided by Natasha Canfer, and for the zest and energy which came with the design skills of McGrath O'Toole, who took our words and gave them the colour and life, and not forgetting the skills and the eye of Stuart Britton Photography.

Barrie Hopson and Mike Scally
Leeds, July 2012